Life in Numbers

Stressed Out!

Michelle R. Prather

Consultants

Diana Herweck, Psy.D.
Clinical Director

Publishing Credits

Rachelle Cracchiolo, M.S.Ed., *Publisher*
Conni Medina, M.A.Ed., *Managing Editor*
Nika Fabienke, Ed.D., *Series Developer*
June Kikuchi, *Content Director*
John Leach, *Assistant Editor*
Lee Aucoin, *Senior Graphic Designer*

TIME For Kids and the TIME For Kids logo are registered trademarks of TIME Inc. Used under license.

Image Credits: Cover and p.1 JGI/Jamie Grill/Getty Images; p.4 Paul D. Stewart/Science Source; all other images from iStock and/or Shutterstock

Library of Congress Cataloging-in-Publication Data

Names: Prather, Michelle Rene?e, 1975- author.
Title: Life in numbers : stressed out! / Michelle R. Prather, M.A.
Description: Huntington Beach, CA : Teacher Created Materials, [2017] | Audience: Grade 4 to 6. | Includes index.
Identifiers: LCCN 2017017376 (print) | LCCN 2017030555 (ebook) | ISBN 9781425853587 (eBook) | ISBN 9781425849849 (pbk.)
Subjects: LCSH: Stress in children--Juvenile literature.
Classification: LCC BF723.S75 (ebook) | LCC BF723.S75 P73 2017 (print) | DDC 155.4/189042--dc23
LC record available at https://lccn.loc.gov/2017017376

Teacher Created Materials
5301 Oceanus Drive
Huntington Beach, CA 92649-1030
http://www.tcmpub.com

ISBN 978-1-4258-4984-9

© 2018 Teacher Created Materials, Inc.
Printed in China
Nordica.022019.CA21900055

Table of Contents

3

What Is Stress?

It is unusual to go a day without hearing someone talk about being stressed. Maybe a parent mentions during dinner that a big work project has been "very stressful." Or you and your friends worry about an upcoming math test. Stress is the body's reaction to certain situations and feelings. It changes how the body functions and how you feel about life—at least temporarily.

Stress sounds…well, stressful! But stress is a normal part of your day, and you should not be afraid of it. Stress can help you protect yourself from threatening **circumstances** and get things done. But too much stress can wear out your body and mind.

Prehistoric Stress

Our ancestors often crossed paths with wild animals. This stress sent adrenaline through their bodies. The adrenaline helped them quickly decide if they should fight or run away.

4

Such a Rush

Adrenaline is one of the hormones released into your bloodstream when you are under pressure. It makes your heart beat faster and your blood pressure rise. It gives you a rush of energy, too.

Are You Stressed Out?

Every day, you **confront** a variety of things that cause stress, even if you do not realize it. You might be unsure of what you are feeling at first. But pay close attention to your body's reactions. These signs can help you **gauge** your stress levels in different situations.

Imagine that you have to present an oral report. If you feel relaxed and confident, you might also feel happy. You know you will get a good grade. Your body and mind feel peaceful. On the other hand, you are definitely *not* at peace if thinking about the report gives you a headache. Signs of stress might include a racing heart, weak knees, or **nausea** (NAH-zhuh).

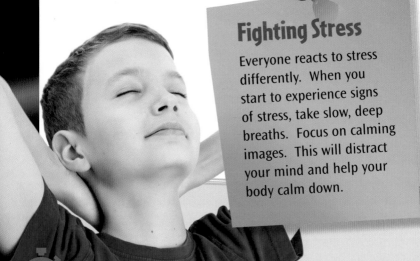

Fighting Stress

Everyone reacts to stress differently. When you start to experience signs of stress, take slow, deep breaths. Focus on calming images. This will distract your mind and help your body calm down.

The State of Stress

If you find yourself feeling stressed a
lot, you are not alone. Many kids are
often stressed. One report showed that
almost one-third of kids suffered a health
problem due to stress in the last month.

Your Body on Stress

Stress can affect your body from head to toe. People who are very sensitive to stress can feel several **symptoms** all at once. Others might feel only one or two. The symptoms can come and go, or they can last until the stressful event has passed.

Some of these pesky red flags your body raises can feel like a cold or the flu. But it is a good idea to ask yourself: "Could I be stressed, rather than sick?" Talk to a parent or guardian about whether you should see a doctor.

Stress Signals

Here are some things to look out for when you are stressed.

headache
dizziness
difficulty focusing

blushing
sweating

clenching teeth
dry mouth

tight muscles

trouble breathing

sweaty palms

nausea

weak legs
leg pain

Measuring Your Mood

There is a handy way to take note of how stressed you are. You can use a number scale just like **psychologists** (sy-KAW-luh-jihsts) who study stress. The scale goes from 1 to 10.

If you are feeling nearly stress-free, you would rate yourself at 1. If you rate yourself between 4 and 7, you are having a stressful day, but this is still in the "normal" range. If your stress level is 8, 9, or 10, you need to take a break. Your body is working overtime to combat the stress. Get some fresh air, stretch your muscles, or talk to a trusted friend. You need to relax in order to function normally again.

The Stress Hormone

Cortisol is a hormone that your body releases when you are stressed. It gives your body a burst of glucose, or sugar. This provides energy. But constant stress creates too much of this hormone—and it could start working against you.

NORMAL
LOW
HIGH
CORTISOL

Going with the Flow

When stress makes your heart race, your entire body gets in on the act. Your breathing is faster, and your lungs take in more oxygen. Blood flow can increase three to four times!

Stress Level: 1–3

Stress Level: 4–7

Stress Level: 8–10

School Stress

Kids spend much of their time at school. This is where a lot of stress can occur. Friendships and grades are often in **flux** and can set off the stress alarm. Being bullied can make you lose sleep at night. Always tell a teacher or another trusted adult if you feel scared or anxious at school.

Things that happen at school can affect you all day, even if they do not seem like a big deal at the time. You might come home from school feeling angry, but you do not know why. Take some time to write or draw about your feelings. When you are able to think a little bit more clearly, talk to an adult about what is bothering you.

Bullying

Bullying can make you feel stressed and scared. It includes repeated pushing, hitting, and teasing. Leaving someone out of a game or starting rumors are also forms of bullying. Bullying is never OK.

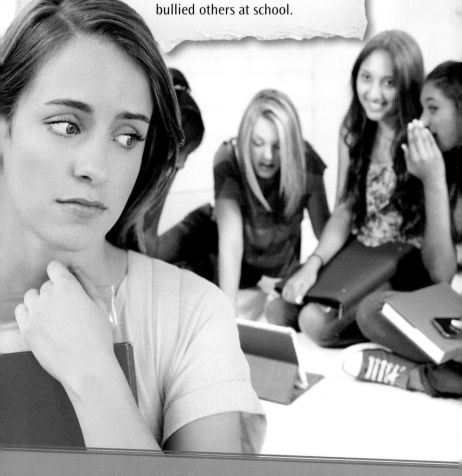

Truth about Bullying

Students in grades 4 through 12 were surveyed about bullying. About half of them had been bullied at school at least once in the past month. And about one-third said they had bullied others at school.

Home Stress

Home is the other place where you probably spend a lot of your time. Even the happiest households have stressful moments. Running late for school or juggling homework and chores can make you tense. A new baby, or even a puppy, can cause stress. Suddenly, what used to be a calm environment is now more exciting…and more stressful!

Just as you cannot control what is happening in the world, you cannot always control what happens in your life. Moving to a new home can throw you off course. Maybe your parents argue a lot, were recently divorced, or are very worried about money. These things, along with everyday events, can create stress.

Stress Survey

Kids between the ages of 8 and 12 were asked about the things in life that cause them stress. Getting along with a sibling caused stress for 14 out of 100 kids. And 28 out of 100 kids said their stress came from worrying about money.

THINK LINK

Psychologists say we're more stressed today than ever before. Are we doing it to ourselves? Let's think about it.

> Technology has made our world very fast paced. Is that good, bad, or somewhere in between?

> How does social media put pressure on kids to keep up with their peers?

> What effect do you think the Internet has on kids' stress levels?

Life Stress

As you grow up, it becomes more common for the world's problems to **seep** into your life. You hear or read about events in the news, and you're aware of more than you were when you were younger. All this new knowledge can begin to weigh you down and make you feel stressed.

It is important to talk to an adult if you are scared about what is going on in the world. Adults can help you understand these events. They can explain why these things are happening. They might even help you think about ways you can change the world for the better!

Survival Mode

You probably will not be chased by tigers. But your body still reacts strongly to less serious things. While walking at the park, if you see a soccer ball flying right at your head, you might duck or move out of the way. This is your body going into survival mode!

Getting Along

Some things are more important to you than others—at least for now. Only 1 out of 20 kids ages 8 to 12 were stressed about their future after graduation from high school. But 4 out of 20 was stressed about their friendships.

Stress Affects Health

Everyone reacts to stress differently. But one thing is certain: too much stress can disrupt the balance of your life. From the time you wake up to the time you fall asleep, being on edge affects your mood.

Losing sleep is one **consequence** of too much stress, and this can become a big problem. If you can't turn off your brain at night, you will not get enough sleep. Without the right amount of sleep, you wake up in a fog. It is harder to remember and cope with things. Paying attention in class and focusing become more difficult, too.

The Right Amount

Want to feel fresh and focused every morning? Doctors agree that the way to do it is to get plenty of sleep! Kids ages 6 to 12 should get 9 to 12 hours of sleep every night.

Tired of It

A study of kids ages 8 to 12 showed some facts about sleep. Around 40 out of 100 had a hard time sleeping. But only 13 out of 100 parents knew that their kids had issues with sleep.

There is also a good chance that your daily nutrition will suffer if you are under too much stress. If stress is making you feel sick to your stomach, you likely will not want to eat. So your first **instinct** at mealtime might be to eat very little or to skip eating.

Sometimes, your stomach may respond to stress in the exact opposite way. A lot of people, kids included, eat when they feel anxious, mad, or even too tired. And most of the time, the food used to "feed the problem" is not healthy. Your body probably will not feel so great after eating all that food. Then, your mind might start to feel bad about it, too. Now you're stressed again!

The Sugar Spike

You now know that your body releases adrenaline and cortisol when it is stressed. Those two hormones make your blood sugar go way up and then way down. After a stressful event, you might feel tired. This is an effect of your blood-sugar levels dropping.

Emotional Eating

Eating while stressed is often called *emotional eating*. Reports say some kids as young as 5 years old head straight for treats to help ease their minds.

Control Your Emotions

It is bad enough when stress affects how you feel. When the way you feel changes how you treat other people, it can cause a different kind of stress. Many kids become moody or start talking back at home when they are under too much pressure. If your parents do not know about your stress, they might scold you for being rude. This could upset you and cause you to talk back even more.

You may even find that your friends suddenly annoy you. You might feel **short-tempered** and mean. Or you may feel so sad that you do not want to hang around the people who usually make you happy.

When you are feeling stressed, take a deep breath and think before you speak. Sometimes, it is best to calmly ask for some time alone. That way, you can get your feelings under control before you say something you might regret.

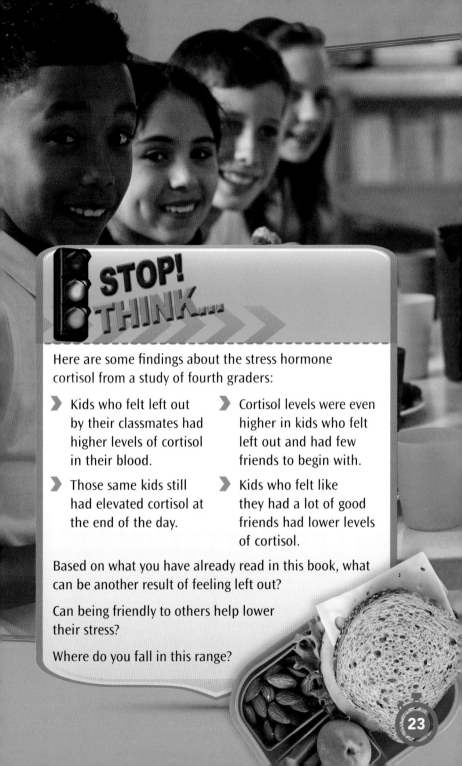

STOP! THINK....

Here are some findings about the stress hormone cortisol from a study of fourth graders:

▶ Kids who felt left out by their classmates had higher levels of cortisol in their blood.

▶ Cortisol levels were even higher in kids who felt left out and had few friends to begin with.

▶ Those same kids still had elevated cortisol at the end of the day.

▶ Kids who felt like they had a lot of good friends had lower levels of cortisol.

Based on what you have already read in this book, what can be another result of feeling left out?

Can being friendly to others help lower their stress?

Where do you fall in this range?

Put a Stop to Stress

Here is the good news: you can stop stress before it gets to you. There are plenty of activities that can **alleviate** stress. Take a walk around your neighborhood with a friend or parent. Listen to music, play an instrument, or do some crafting. Play a game, run in place, or have a dance party in your living room. Or just do something nice for someone. All these activities help by taking your mind off of whatever is making you stressed!

Try learning about deep breathing and **meditation**. When you breathe from your stomach, your heart rate decreases. By slowing down, you can start to relax. *Aahhh!*

School Meditation

Students at a Maryland school have a special room where they can go when they are feeling stressed. The "Meditation Room" is a quiet place where kids can stretch, do yoga, and calm down.

Scrunch Up Stress!

Grab a magazine or newspaper from your recycling bin and get to work relieving stress. Assign a worry or **woe** to each page, and then crumple it up. Imagine you are throwing that stress away as you toss each ball back into the recycle bin.

Enough Is Enough!

Now that you know stress can be squashed, it is a good time to make this promise. Tell yourself, "Stress will not get the best of me."

You will always have to deal with minor stresses. Your heart will still beat more quickly if you see a strange dog running toward you, and your face may still feel hot and get sweaty when you are embarrassed. But now you know some strategies you can use to overcome stress.

The more we learn about coping with stress, the better we will get along. Imagine if we all took a few deep breaths more often. We would be a happier, healthier, and more peaceful society.

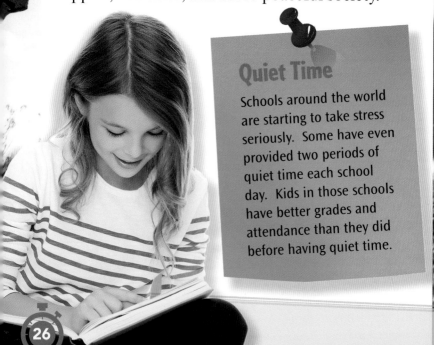

Quiet Time

Schools around the world are starting to take stress seriously. Some have even provided two periods of quiet time each school day. Kids in those schools have better grades and attendance than they did before having quiet time.

Work It Out

Exercise is one great way to relieve stress. And it helps keep your body healthy, too. Exercising is good for your body and your mind, so get active!

Glossary

alleviate—make something less painful or troubling

circumstances—conditions

confront—to face something or somebody; to come up against

consequence—the result of something

flux—a constant state of change

gauge—to figure out and make a judgment about something

instinct—a behavior that is automatic

meditation—the act of clearing the mind in a quiet setting

nausea—the feeling of needing to vomit

psychologists—experts in behavior and the mind

seep—to pass slowly through something

short-tempered—easily made angry

symptoms—signs of something bad

woe—something that causes a problem

Index

Check It Out!

Books

Lynch, Christopher. 2012. *Totally Chill: My Complete Guide to Staying Cool.* AAPC Publishing.

Moss, Wendy L. 2015. *Bounce Back: How to Be a Resilient Kid.* Magination Press.

Romain, Trevor, and Elizabeth Verdick. 2005. *Stress Can Really Get on Your Nerves!* Free Spirit Publishing.

Shapiro, Lawrence E., and Robin K. Sprague. 2009. *The Relaxation and Stress Reduction Workbook for Kids: Help for Children to Cope with Stress, Anxiety, and Transitions.* Instant Help.

Websites

Common Sense Media. "Meditation Apps for Kids." www.commonsensemedia.org/lists/meditation-apps-for-kids.

PBS Kids. "It's My Life." www.pbskids.org/itsmylife/.

Try It!

Do you feel lower, grumpier, or more stressed than usual? Figure out what is going on by keeping a log! Log the low parts of your day, and write the best word to describe how you feel. This can help you see the big picture. Writing down the time of day is also useful. That way, you can look for patterns about when you are being pushed to your limit. After keeping a log for a while, you may notice a decrease in your times of stress. If not, go back to pages 24 and 25 for some handy tips on how to relax.

Here is a sample chart to give you an idea of how to start your log:

What Bugged Me Today

Time	What Happened	I Felt...
6:30 a.m.	I spilled my cereal.	worried/frustrated
9:00 a.m.	I realized I forgot my math homework.	panicked
10:30 a.m.	Ian bragged about his new phone.	jealous
12:30 p.m.	Tatiana made fun of me in front of everyone.	angry/embarrassed
3:00 p.m.	Dad was late to pick me up.	anxious
6:00 p.m.	I still wasn't finished with homework.	tired/frustrated

About the Author

Michelle R. Prather is a longtime writer and editor. She got her start interviewing business owners and telling their stories in magazines. Since then, she has written guided planners and journals, edited young adult novels, and coauthored an art book. She started college as a dance major, but she ended up with degrees in film studies and history. Her big dreams include opening the best-ever children's bookstore and writing a fiction series her daughter would love.

Tech World

The Language of
SOCIAL MEDIA

Christine Dugan, M.A.

Publishing Credits

Rachelle Cracchiolo, M.S.Ed., *Publisher*
Conni Medina, M.A.Ed., *Managing Editor*
Nika Fabienke, Ed.D., *Series Developer*
June Kikuchi, *Content Director*
Seth Rogers, *Editor*
Michelle Jovin, M.A., *Assistant Editor*
Lee Aucoin, *Senior Graphic Designer*

TIME For Kids and the TIME For Kids logo are registered trademarks of TIME Inc. Used under license.

Image Credits: p.20 Behrouz Mehri/AFP/Getty Images; all other images from iStock and/or Shutterstock.

Library of Congress Cataloging-in-Publication Data

Names: Dugan, Christine, author.
Title: Tech world : the language of social media / Christine Dugan, M.A.
Description: Huntington Beach, CA : Teacher Created Materials, [2017] | Includes index.
Identifiers: LCCN 2017023526 (print) | LCCN 2017024942 (ebook) | ISBN 9781425854652 (eBook) | ISBN 9781425849894 (pbk.)
Subjects: LCSH: Communication--Technological innovations--Juvenile literature. | Social media--Juvenile literature. | Mass media--Computer network resources--Juvenile literature. | Internet--Juvenile literature. | Mass media--Social aspects--Juvenile literature.
Classification: LCC P91.28 (ebook) | LCC P91.28 .D94 2017 (print) | DDC 302.23--dc23
LC record available at https://lccn.loc.gov/2017023526

Teacher Created Materials

5301 Oceanus Drive
Huntington Beach, CA 92649-1030
http://www.tcmpub.com

ISBN 978-1-4258-4989-4

© 2018 Teacher Created Materials, Inc.
Made in China
Nordica.092017.CA21701119

Table of Contents

Get the Word Out

Imagine that your soccer team won the league championship. It was an awesome game, and you scored the winning goal! How can you tell your friends about your big win? You could wait until the next time you see them. Sending a group text is another way to share news.

You could also use **social media** to get the word out quickly. Social media allows people to share words and pictures that describe what is happening in their lives. It makes communication easier. It also helps someone share news with many people at once. Social media is a fairly new way to share information. People need to learn *how* to communicate on social media.

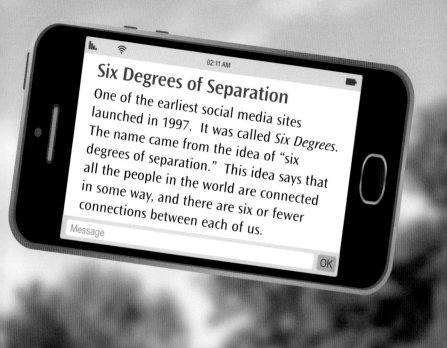

Six Degrees of Separation

One of the earliest social media sites launched in 1997. It was called *Six Degrees*. The name came from the idea of "six degrees of separation." This idea says that all the people in the world are connected in some way, and there are six or fewer connections between each of us.

Message   OK

What Is It?

The term *social media* is used to describe types of electronic communication. It is the way people share information online. They can share their thoughts, photos, images, or videos by **posting** them for others to see.

A New Kind of Language

Speech on social media is not the same as speech in person. It is not the same as writing a note or an email. Social media has its own unique "language." And it keeps growing because social media is so popular. People need to keep up with how to "talk" in this new way.

Social media users often make up words. They also give old words new meanings. **Abbreviated** words and **acronyms** are popular among users. Even pictures mean things on social media! It can be hard to keep up with all the changes.

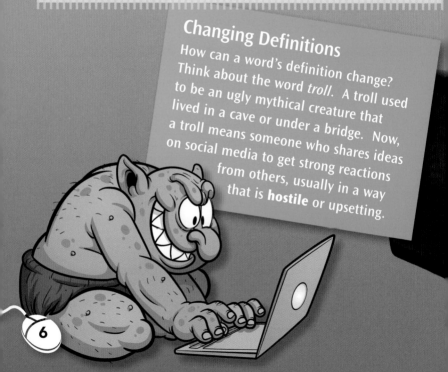

Changing Definitions

How can a word's definition change? Think about the word *troll*. A troll used to be an ugly mythical creature that lived in a cave or under a bridge. Now, a troll means someone who shares ideas on social media to get strong reactions from others, usually in a way that is **hostile** or upsetting.

APP

UNFRIEND

BLOG

WiFi

02:11 AM

What Is That Word?

Social media has introduced words that never existed before. One invented word that quickly took off is *selfie*. Now, everyone knows that this word means to take a quick picture of yourself.

essage

OK

Changing Language

This shift in language is not unique to social media. The words we use are always changing and **evolving**. Sometimes change happens so slowly that it's hard to notice; at other times, it seems to happen overnight! But why does language change? One reason is that it must meet the needs of the people who use it, and since people change over time, so does language.

Scientists have studied how those changes happen. One way is that inventions and technology often require new words. Social media is simply a new experience that comes with a new set of vocabulary.

Google It!

The Google™ **search engine** is so popular that people have started using its name as a verb—to *Google* something. Have you ever heard someone say, "I don't know, just Google it"? The term was used so often that it was added to the dictionary. That was not welcome news for Google (the company), since they ask that people never use it in that way!

The Rise of New Languages

As civilizations grow, so do languages. New words and symbols express ideas in new ways. Here are some examples of new languages that have developed over time.

4300 BC
hieroglyphics

3000 BC
cuneiform language

2650 BC
Chinese alphabet

730
Greek alphabet

900
Latin

1600
cursive alphabet

1900
binary code

present day
social media

Many people study social media. They watch the effects it has on people. Changes in language tend to happen much faster today than they did in the past. That is because social media connects people all around the world. A new word or phrase can spread very quickly. One person can start a new **trend**. Often, people do not know who starts these new words.

Social Media Age Restrictions

must be **13** to be on:	**14**	LinkedIn
Twitter® Facebook® Instagram Pinterest Google+® Tumblr Reddit® Snapchat	**16**	WhatsApp®
	18	Path®
	18 or 13 with parent permission	YouTube, WeChat®, Foursquare®, Flickr®

Lies vs. The Truth

Many people think that lies spread faster than the truth. As the old saying goes, "A lie can travel halfway around the world while the truth is putting on its shoes."

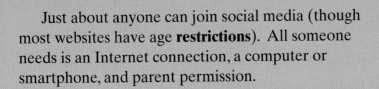

Just about anyone can join social media (though most websites have age **restrictions**). All someone needs is an Internet connection, a computer or smartphone, and parent permission.

02:11 AM

Radio Days

It took 38 years for the radio to reach 50 million users. More people than that were using Facebook just three years after its launch.

Message

OK

Social Media Talk

Social media communication tends to be informal. That means it is casual and friendly. Users do not use the same words that they would in speeches or presentations. People have certain expectations for the way things are written on social media.

Sharing on social media is quick and easy. It's part of the experience. That is where the "social" **aspect** comes into play. Users want to be heard. And they usually want a response from others about the things they have posted.

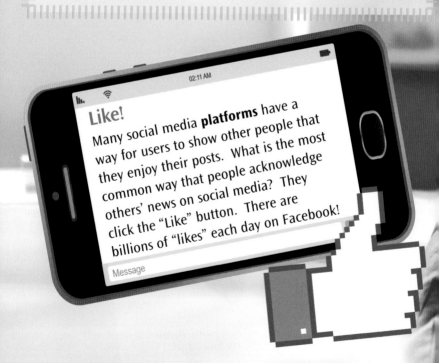

02:11 AM

Like!

Many social media **platforms** have a way for users to show other people that they enjoy their posts. What is the most common way that people acknowledge others' news on social media? They click the "Like" button. There are billions of "likes" each day on Facebook!

Message

"best tacos n the wrld @ jake's rn omg"

"I just had a wonderful dinner at my friend, Jacob's house. Wow, those tacos certainly were delicious!"

Think Twice, Post Once

Many people make the mistake of thinking their social media posts are private. But it is important to keep in mind that there are records of all social media exchanges. You should always think twice before you post!

Social Media Shorthand

Abbreviations and acronyms are forms of social media communication. Users rely on them to send out quick thoughts or responses. If people see a funny image online, they do not have to type, "That is so funny; it made me laugh!" Instead, users can type, "LOL!" (laughing out loud!).

Abbreviations also help on websites that require you to be brief. For example, Twitter has a rule on how long posts can be. It does not allow users to type more than 140 **characters** in a single post. Abbreviations help users send long messages in a short way.

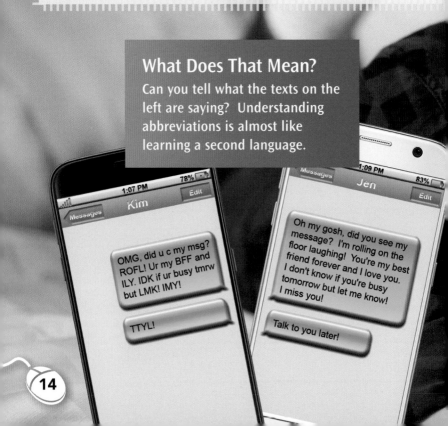

What Does That Mean?

Can you tell what the texts on the left are saying? Understanding abbreviations is almost like learning a second language.

OMG, did u c my msg? ROFL! Ur my BFF and ILY. IDK if ur busy tmrw but LMK! IMY!

TTYL!

Oh my gosh, did you see my message? I'm rolling on the floor laughing! You're my best friend forever and I love you. I don't know if you're busy tomorrow but let me know! I miss you!

Talk to you later!

JK, ILY!

Social media is full of initialisms. They are formed by using the first letters of the words in a phrase instead of saying the whole words. TBH (to be honest), IDC (I don't care), and ILY (I love you) are all initialisms.

ROFL

CUL8R

ILY

ASAP

When speaking with others, people must use some kind of common language. Abbreviations and acronyms are no different. Social media users have to understand them in order to communicate.

The abbreviations you use may depend on why you are online. If someone sends you a sweet birthday message, you could respond with, "THX 4 ur msg!" (Thanks for your message!). Or, maybe you want to plan to have lunch with a friend. You might ask when you can see your BFF (best friend forever) IRL (in real life).

02:11 AM

I'll Text You

Some of the language of social media has made its way into use outside social media. Texters might talk about funny GIFs (graphics interchange format) they sent. And if someone tells you to "keep it on the DL," that means to keep it on the down low (keep it secret).

OK

Message

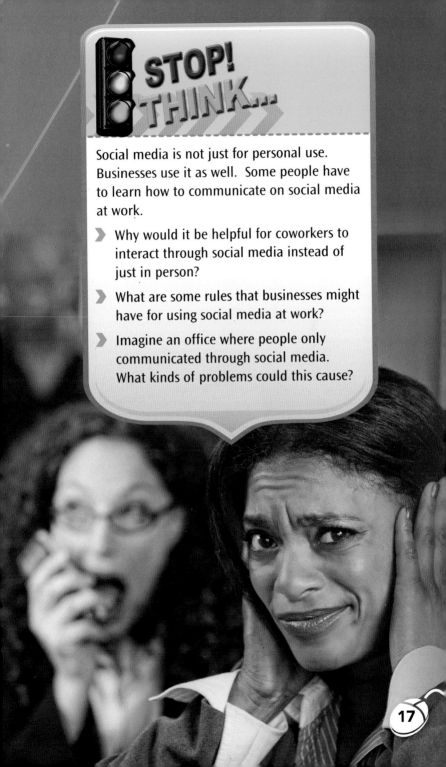

STOP! THINK...

Social media is not just for personal use. Businesses use it as well. Some people have to learn how to communicate on social media at work.

- ❯ Why would it be helpful for coworkers to interact through social media instead of just in person?

- ❯ What are some rules that businesses might have for using social media at work?

- ❯ Imagine an office where people only communicated through social media. What kinds of problems could this cause?

Emoji

Abbreviations are not the only way to shorten a post. You can also use small pictures called *emoji*.

Emoji are very popular on social media. They help users share how they are feeling about different topics. An emoji can add a unique **tone** to a message. Instead of just sharing a sad or happy face, an emoji can share more **complex** feelings. That way, you could tell if someone is feeling scared, shy, or furious.

Emoji are also a fun and quick way to react to news. A thumbs up or a happy face can say just as much as typing, "I like that" or "Way to go!"

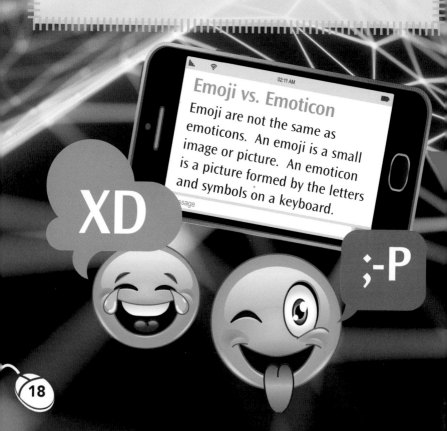

Emoji vs. Emoticon

Emoji are not the same as emoticons. An emoji is a small image or picture. An emoticon is a picture formed by the letters and symbols on a keyboard.

XD

;-P

What Does It Mean?

Emoji were invented in Japan in 1999. The word *emoji* comes from two Japanese words: *e* means "picture" and *moji* means "character."

THE HISTORY OF EMOJI

Shigetaka Kurita (shih-geh-TAH-kuh koo-REE-tuh) is the inventor of emoji.

1999: Emoji were first designed. Kurita used pictures shown in a weather forecast as the basis for the first emoji.

Kurita had to develop the first 180 emoji in just one month!

Emoji were black and white at first. They later came in color.

Emoji were first designed for people in Japan only. Kurita is very surprised by how common they are now.

What is the future of emoji? Kurita thinks that people will develop more specific and local emoji that better represent their own communities.

Hashtags

Social media users also share ideas by using hashtags. These are keywords or phrases that are written after the hash symbol (#). People can include them in social media posts. The hashtag then acts as a **hyperlink**. Users can click on the link, and they will see other posts about the same topic.

Hashtags are usually placed at the end of a post. But they can be used at the beginning or in the middle, too. How do they help us communicate? Hashtags give us related information. They also help us organize our ideas into categories.

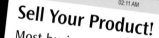

02:11 AM

Sell Your Product!

Most businesses use social media platforms. Hashtags can help guide customers to different posts that are related to their products. This can be a useful way to get the word out about what a business is selling.

Message

OK

BOWLING
TOURNAMENT
#BOWLERAMA

GRAND PRIZE!
COME JOIN US!

$15
ENTRY

#Bowlerama #BirthdayBowling
#StrikesAllDayAllNight #UJelly
#LoveMyFriends #BFFs

#Hashtag

Some people use hashtags for a different reason. They might add hashtags to express their opinions about posts. They can make their posts #funny, #serious, or #sarcastic.

The Shorter the Better?

Do people really need to use short words or pictures to get messages across? Many users think so. After all, people are talking through screens. A user might not understand everything about a message. So emoji and abbreviated messages help users. They can show more about what is being said. They can also help users read between the lines.

Beware of Ghosts

02:11 AM

The best way to learn the language of social media is to be online. Some people have social media accounts, but are never active on them. These people are called *ghosts*. Almost half of the people who are on Twitter are ghosts who have never sent a tweet.

Message

OK

As people spend more time online and on social media, they begin to recognize the language. After awhile, they no longer need to stop and think about what it all means. In this way, many social media users become **bilingual**.

No Words Allowed!

Some social media websites require users to *only* communicate with emoji. The idea has not spread quite yet, but you never know!

That Is Not What I Meant!

Sometimes, when people talk, there can be errors in communication. They might misunderstand each other. Or, each side might hear the same conversation in very different ways. This is true when people talk face-to-face. And it is definitely true on social media.

Social media language can be open to **interpretation**. People understand ideas in their own ways. They may not be clear about someone else's meaning. There are no **facial expressions** to read. There is no body language to read. There is no tone of voice to consider. Mistakes happen!

So Many Faces!

Consider how many emoji we have for showing our emotions. Some of the images look very similar. Do you think it might be easy to confuse what someone is trying to say? How?

Can you think of a time when someone misunderstood something you said? It happens to everyone. How might these different groups of people interpret the same social media post?

> adults and teenagers

> men and women

> people in different countries

How might these issues be avoided by speaking in person?

Connecting with Others

Social media helps us to connect with others. People can see messages from users all around the world in an instant. Is this a good thing? Is using this new social media language always positive?

Positive Connections

Users on social media can make many positive connections. They can keep in touch with people who are close to them. They can share messages and news with their loved ones. They can even connect with people they haven't seen in years. Social media is a quick and easy way for people to communicate.

Fast Fingers

In 2014, a 17-year-old boy set a new world record. Marcel Fernandes Filho typed a long text message in just 18 seconds. His speed made him the "World's Fastest Texter." What did he type?

The razor-toothed piranhas of the genera Serrasalmus and Pygocentrus are the most ferocious freshwater fish in the world. In reality they seldom attack a human.

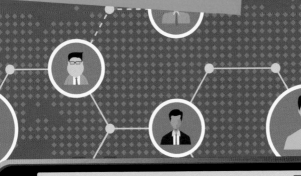

lı.   ᯤ   02:11 AM

Join the Club!

More than two billion people use social media. The number continues to grow each day! Many people use their cell phones to view their accounts. Some estimates show that every second, 12 people use their cell phones to open new social media accounts.

Message   OK

Raising Awareness

In a poll, 4 out of 10 teens said that social media has made them more aware of the needs of others. The studies also showed that more girls "liked" charities online than boys.

Being on social media also gives people a chance to help others. Many people use social media to write about ways to support **causes** that are important to them. Some users ask their friends to donate money. Others ask people to sign **petitions**.

Social media makes our world feel smaller. Since we all speak a common language online, users start to think about people in other places. They can hear about what life is like for others. This kind of connection makes people want to help others in need.

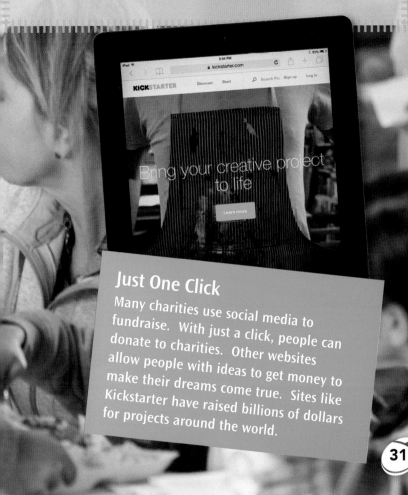

Just One Click

Many charities use social media to fundraise. With just a click, people can donate to charities. Other websites allow people with ideas to get money to make their dreams come true. Sites like Kickstarter have raised billions of dollars for projects around the world.

Negative Connections

Social media language can be negative, too. Sometimes, people share unkind things about others. These mean comments can spread quickly. It can be hurtful if you are the subject of these cruel posts.

Before you post something, stop and think. Is your online message something you would say in person? If the answer is no, it is probably not okay to share it online. You should also ask yourself how you would feel if someone posted your message about you. If you think it would hurt your feelings, keep the mean thought to yourself.

02:11 AM

Don't Be a Bully!

If a person bothers someone online, it is called *cyberbullying*. It is just like bullying in real life, except it happens online. It can happen through mean messages, fake profiles, or sending unwanted photos.

Message

Report It!

Some kids don't report being bullied because it makes them feel ashamed, afraid, and powerless. Others worry that it will cause them to lose friends. After a while, they may begin to feel like they deserve to be bullied. If you or someone you know has been cyberbullied, tell an adult who you trust right away.

Protect Your Privacy

Privacy settings are different for each website. It is important to know who can see what you are sharing in order to stay safe online. Basic rules are to keep your name, age, and address private. You should also be careful about posting where you are, especially if you do not know all of your friends or followers.

02:11 AM

Message

OK

Staying Safe on Social Media

A key rule of social media is the same as a key rule in life: treat others how you want to be treated. Just because users are connecting through a screen does not change the rules. Always remind yourself to keep things positive.

You—and your parents—should also be aware of your privacy settings. These settings are not the same on all social media sites. Make sure that you know what information is visible to others and who can see it. And never share passwords with anyone!

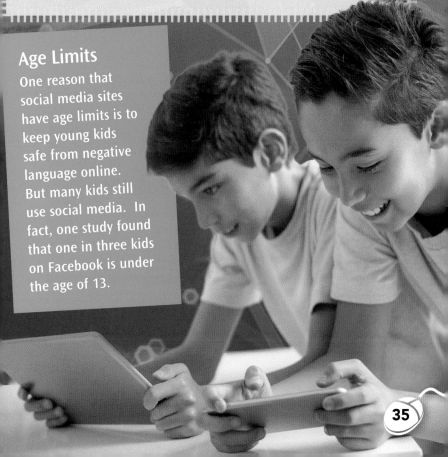

Age Limits

One reason that social media sites have age limits is to keep young kids safe from negative language online. But many kids still use social media. In fact, one study found that one in three kids on Facebook is under the age of 13.

Changing the Dictionary

The language of social media changes quickly. Some words stick and become a part of daily language. Other words are a **fad** and soon drop off.

Some social media words have made their way into the dictionary. New words are added to dictionaries as they become more popular. In recent years, many of these new words deal with technology. Before that, people might not have known what they meant. Once they are in the dictionary, everyone has access to the language.

Making It Official

The Oxford English Dictionary (OED) is a huge collection of words. When the authors first wrote the dictionary, it took them five years to reach the word *ant*! Since 2004, the OED picks a Word of the Year. Some of the words they have chosen include "podcast," "unfriend," "GIF," and "selfie." In 2015, the Word of the Year was not a word—it was the emoji shown above!

Words That Last

Researchers who work for the OED **track** new words. They want to see evidence that a word is used for about 10 years before it is added to the dictionary. Sometimes, they do not wait that long. But they want to make sure that a word is not just a fad. They want to make sure the word will continue to be **relevant** and useful.

blog *(BLAHG) noun*

A regularly updated website or web page run by an individual or small group that is written in an informal or conversational style.

meme *(MEEM) noun*

An image, video, piece of text, etc., typically humorous in nature, that is copied and spread rapidly by Internet users, often with slight variations.

tweet *(TWEET) noun*

A post made on the social media application twitter.

Wi-Fi *(WIGH-figh) noun*

A facility allowing computers or other devices to connect to the Internet wirelessly within a particular area.

Source: Oxford English Dictionary

New Technology Words

The language of social media is spreading rapidly. Sometimes it can be hard to keep up with all of the new words and meanings. Do you know what these words mean when they are used in the context of social media? Do you know anybody who might have trouble answering the following questions?

1. Someone tells you they found a hilarious *GIF*. What did they find?

   A. a message sent on social media
   B. a new acronym for "Great, I forgot!"
   C. multiple images put together to look like a video

2. Before social media, you had to go outside and find a bird to hear a *tweet*. Where do you go to tweet someone now?

   A. Twitter
   B. Tumblr
   C. Tagged

3. If a friend says they are *streaming* something, what are they doing?

   A. standing in a narrow flow of water
   B. watching a video or listening to audio over the Internet
   C. moving in a smooth direction

4. Your mom tells you that she just *stumbled upon* something online. What did she do?

   A. She tripped over something.
   B. She found it hard to say something.
   C. She discovered something new.

5. If someone makes you into a *meme*, what did they do?

   A. made your image into a funny picture
   B. wrote a blog entry about you
   C. turned your name into an acronym

Answers: 1. C; 2. A; 3. B; 4. C; 5. A

Join the Conversation?

Social media can be exciting. It allows you to stay in touch with friends and family. It lets you share the things that are going on in your life. You can also comment on what is happening in the world. Many people find social media to be positive and friendly.

Now that you know some of the ways that social media users communicate, how would you post about winning that big soccer game? Would you find the perfect emoji to capture your excitement? Or would you use acronyms?

Keep learning the language of social media, and let people know about your day. After all, YOLO (you only live once)!

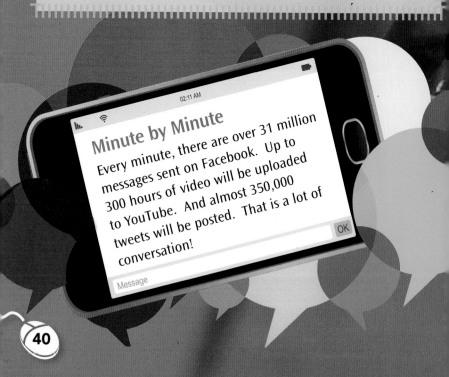

02:11 AM

Minute by Minute

Every minute, there are over 31 million messages sent on Facebook. Up to 300 hours of video will be uploaded to YouTube. And almost 350,000 tweets will be posted. That is a lot of conversation!

OK

Message

Around the World

In 1990, there were just three million Internet users. By 2015, there were more than three billion! Even with the quick spread, over half of the world still does not have access to the Internet.

Glossary

abbreviated—made shorter

acronyms—words formed from the first letter or letters of words in phrases

aspect—part of something

bilingual—able to speak and understand two languages

causes—organizations, beliefs, ideas, or goals that people support

characters—letters, numbers, or punctuation marks

complex—not easy to understand or explain

evolving—changing over time

facial expressions—the act of showing feelings or emotions with your face

fad—something that is very popular but only for a short period of time

hostile—showing or having unfriendly feelings

hyperlink—a highlighted word or image in a document or on a website that takes you to another location in the same document or to a website

interpretation—the act of understanding something in a particular way

petitions—formal requests that people sign to show they want people or organizations to change or do something

platforms—places that allow people to convey information to larger groups of people

posting—writing and sending a message online

relevant—having to do with a certain topic

restrictions—laws or rules that control something

search engine—a computer program used to find information on the Internet

social media—different forms of electronic communication that allow users to share information and create communities online

tone—a feeling or attitude that is expressed by the words a person uses while writing or speaking

track—to follow the path of something

trend—something that is popular at a given time

Index

Check It Out!

Books

MacEachern, Robyn. 2010. *Cyberbullying: Deal with it and Ctrl Alt Delete it.* Lorimer.

Palacio, R. J. 2012. *Wonder.* Knopf Books for Young Readers.

Polacco, Patricia. 2012. *Bully.* G.P. Putnam's Sons Books for Young Readers.

Taylor, Chloe. 2013. *Stitches and Stones.* Simon Spotlight.

Websites

Internet Safety 101. www.internetsafety101.org

PACER Center, Inc. *Pacer Center's Kids Against Bullying.* www.pacerkidsagainstbullying.org/kab/

SlangIt. *Social Media Slang.* www.slangit.com/terms/social_media

Stopbullying.gov. www.stopbullying.gov

Try It!

Your school wants to create a social media website for students to communicate. The principal has asked you to be in charge!

👍 Design a symbol for your website, and choose a color scheme.

👍 Label the different sections of your website. Will there be an area for homework help or school event information?

👍 Create emoji that students can use, maybe a person with a heart beating out of his or her chest to use when they are excited about the school graduation party. What about a pirate eye patch to use when students think an idea sounds cool?

👍 Write an "About Us" page that gives a brief description of your school.

👍 Draw your homepage, complete with your symbol at the top and a catchy motto.

About the Author

Christine Dugan has written many books for both students and teachers. She has worked as an author, an editor, and a classroom teacher. Currently, Dugan teaches in the Pacific Northwest, where she lives with her husband and their two daughters. She loves to communicate with her friends and family using social media. Dugan is always sure to include many emoji so they know how she is *really* feeling!

CELL PHONE
Pros and Cons

Lesley Ward

Publishing Credits

Rachelle Cracchiolo, M.S.Ed., *Publisher*
Conni Medina, M.A.Ed., *Managing Editor*
Nika Fabienke, Ed.D., *Series Developer*
June Kikuchi, *Content Director*
John Leach, *Assistant Editor*
Lee Aucoin, *Senior Graphic Designer*

TIME For Kids and the TIME For Kids logo are registered trademarks of TIME Inc. Used under license.

Image Credits: p.8 Simon Rawles/Getty Images; all other images from iStock and/or Shutterstock

Teacher Created Materials
5301 Oceanus Drive
Huntington Beach, CA 92649-1030
http://www.tcmpub.com
ISBN 978-1-4258-4977-1
© 2018 Teacher Created Materials, Inc.
Printed in China
Nordica.122018.CA21801488

Table of Contents

Connect to the World

People use their cell phones for many different reasons. They talk, send texts, take pictures, listen to music, and play games on their phones. They even use their cell phones to shop. The next time you are in a crowd, look around. Would you be surprised to see that most people are holding cell phones?

In some countries, many people do not have computers. They use their cell phones to browse the Internet. Phones that have these **capabilities** are called *smartphones*.

In the past, cell phones were very expensive, so only adults had them. But today many kids have their own phones. Owning a phone is a big responsibility—for kids and adults!

Get Mobile

The term *cell phone* comes from the way a phone works. Every phone links to a tower that is in the middle of an area called a *cell*. In some places, a cell phone is called a mobile phone.

I Need My Phone!

Some people worry a lot about being without their cell phones. Now there is even a special word to describe this feeling: *nomophobia*! This is a short version of "no mobile phone **phobia**."

Message

5

The Computer in Your Hand

A cell phone is a miniature computer. That means all the **components** inside the phone are miniature in size, too. Tiny microphones, microchips, and antennas fit inside the phone. Little transmitters and receivers send and receive signals.

Most people are not interested in how their cell phones work. They only care that their phones work when they need them. And people rely on their cell phones all the time. They use their phones as alarm clocks to wake them up. They look up stuff on the Internet, pay bills, and play games on their phones. Cell phones are truly amazing!

Watch That Phone

A smartwatch connects to your cell phone and to the Internet. It acts like a remote control. When you select apps on your smartwatch, it sends messages to your cell phone.

The First Cell Phone

The first cell phone was big. It weighed just under two pounds and was 13 inches tall. It was too heavy to carry around for very long. It was also expensive—it cost almost $4,000! Not many people could afford one.

Cell phones are built using many tiny parts.

Cell Phones Around the World

There are some places where people do not have access to computers. They use cell phones instead. They send messages to friends. They catch up on news and check the weather. Cell phones connect people to the rest of the world.

In Mexico, doctors use cell phones to send messages to patients and remind them to take their medicine. In Pakistan, farmers receive texts that tell them when to plant vegetables. In many African countries, people who don't have access to banks use their phones to track their money. Cell phones can help kids and adults around the world have better lives.

Caring for Cows

In Kenya, many farmers use their cell phones to keep their **livestock** healthy. Some use an app called iCow. It gives farmers advice about caring for their cows, chickens, sheep, and goats.

Message

OK

Flashlight in a Phone

In some places, many streets are poorly lit or without power. It can be scary to walk around after dark. The flashlight feature on most cell phones can light the way!

Safety Issues

Most kids use their cell phones to stay in touch with friends. They rarely think about their phones in terms of safety. But one of the main reasons parents let their kids have phones is safety.

In case of an emergency, you can call to get help right away. If you get lost or hurt, you can use your cell phone to call someone in your family. If you see an accident, you can contact the police.

This is all common sense, but sometimes people freeze during an emergency. **Panic** is a natural reaction. But it's important to remain calm and call for help. That's what cell phones are for!

ICE

It's a good idea to put an ICE (In Case of Emergency) contact in your phone. A person who helps you in an emergency will know to call this number right away. For example, you could store parents' numbers as "ICE Mom" and "ICE Dad."

GPS Tracking

Most modern cell phones can use GPS (Global Positioning System). This is a tracking system that lets you know where the phone is located. And if you call the police in an emergency, your phone will tell them where you are.

OK

Message

Put Down the Phone

Some people spend too much time on their phones. They talk, text, and play games all day long with few breaks. When they feel bored, lonely, or worried, they pick up their phones. They're on their phones while watching television or doing homework. They even check their phones while driving, which is dangerous and against the law! These people have cell phone **addiction**.

Spending too much time on your cell phone is bad for your body and mind. Looking down at your phone screen for long periods of time can make your eyes tired and can hurt your back and neck. Using a phone before bedtime can make it hard to fall asleep. And not sleeping enough makes you tired and grouchy. Scientists discovered that cell phones give off small amounts of electrical waves called *radiation*. What does all this mean? People should limit their cell phone use.

Phones on Fire

A cell phone company made headlines in 2016. Some of its phones burst into flames. The phones had **defective** batteries that exploded when they became too hot. The company **recalled** millions of phones to keep phone users safe.

Message

OK

Loaded with Germs

Cell phones often have more germs and bacteria on them than toilet seats. Yuck! Germs can make you sick. Everyone should **disinfect** their cell phones regularly. Washing your hands before handling your phone is a good idea, too.

13

Fun with Cell Phones

Everywhere you go, people use their cell phones. They talk on their phones while walking down the street. They watch videos while sitting on a train. They check their email and texts while eating in a restaurant. It's strange to think that so many people do these things in public.

People also use the cameras on their phones. They take photos and videos of themselves and their friends. Sometimes, they post a funny photo or video on the Internet, and millions of people watch it. This is called *going viral*.

What if someone posted a photo or a video of you online? What if you were doing something embarrassing? Would you like it? Probably not!

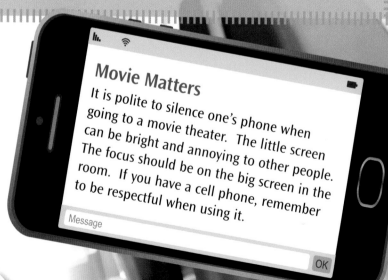

Movie Matters

It is polite to silence one's phone when going to a movie theater. The little screen can be bright and annoying to other people. The focus should be on the big screen in the room. If you have a cell phone, remember to be respectful when using it.

Message

OK

STOP! THINK...

> Can you think of places where using a cell phone is a bad idea?
> Should you be allowed to use a cell phone at school? Why or why not?
> No one likes it when people talk loudly on their phones in public. When you have to make a call in public, how can you show respect to those around you?

Personalized Cell Phones

Most people use their cell phones to show off their style. They choose a cool-looking phone case or cover. Luckily, cases and covers come in a lot of different colors and designs. Cell phones are **fragile**, so cases not only make phones look good, but they also offer protection.

Another way people personalize their phones is with the wallpaper, or the background on the main screen. Most people do not use the selection of patterns and photos that comes with the phone. Instead, they use a photo with people, animals, or sports logos. The best thing is that wallpapers can be changed anytime.

People can also select different ringtones for their cellphones. You may hear phones ring, buzz, or quack. Some phones sound like bells or crashing ocean waves. Popular songs can even be **downloaded** as ringtones.

quack, quack

buzz, buzz

Good Vibrations

If you are in a quiet place, such as a library, you don't want your phone to bother other people. Switch the phone to "vibrate," and your phone will shake when you get a call.

Message | OK

Wet Phone? Try Rice!

Thousands of cell phones are dropped in water each year. If your phone isn't waterproof, what can you do? Try drying out your phone in rice! Remove the battery from your phone. Place the battery and your phone in a bowl of rice. Leave them in the bowl overnight. The rice often absorbs the water. If you're lucky, your phone may work in the morning.

ALL ABOUT THE APPS

App is short for *application*. It is a software program for your phone. You open apps by simply touching their **icons** on your phone screen. There are thousands of apps. Apps can be games, magazines, or newspapers. They can help you keep track of what you eat or stay in contact with friends. Many apps are free. Check out some types of apps that you can download on your phone.

Educational apps teach subjects such as math or science.

Television and movie apps let you watch your favorite shows on your phone.

Map apps tell you where you are and give you directions.

Game apps let you test your skills and battle your friends!

Weather apps tell you the forecast and the current outside temperature.

Social media apps connect you to your friends and family.

Music apps let you listen to your favorite tunes any time you want.

19

Kids and Cell Phones

Adults have different **opinions** on when their child should have a cell phone. All kids are different, so there is no perfect age to get a phone. It depends on how responsible you are.

Do you regularly break stuff or lose things like your homework? Do you have a hard time remembering where you put your belongings? If this sounds like you, don't be surprised if your parents say that you are not ready for a cell phone.

Your parents will likely make rules about your cell phone use. It's important to follow these rules because it shows that you can handle the responsibility of having a phone. One rule might be that you can use your cell phone only for a short amount of time each day.

Cell Phone Contract

You can show that you are responsible. Create a cell phone contract. Make a list of rules for phone use, and sign it. This will show that you are serious about owning a phone.

THINK LINK

Having your own cell phone is a **privilege**. Not every kid has a cell phone. If you have one, you must take care of it.

- How can a kid prove that he or she is ready to have a phone?
- What kind of rules might come with a cell phone?
- Do you think you are ready to have a phone? Why, or why not?

Cell phones come with some handy features. For example, most smartphone screens automatically lock. This stops people from using your phone without your permission. Your phone won't open until you tap in a special passcode. Only you and your parents should know your passcode.

If you are unable to answer your phone, an incoming call will go to your voicemail box. Record a voicemail greeting so the caller can leave a message. Most people say something such as, "Sorry I missed your call. I will call you back." You can be creative with your voicemail greeting, but make sure your parents approve of the one you make.

If it's all right with your parents, download some fun apps for your phone. Ask your friends about their favorite apps.

Where's My Phone?

Cell phones come with apps that help you find your phone if you lose it. You can simply sign in to a website that will locate your missing phone. It will show you the phone's location on a map.

Be Smart on Your Phone

It's a good idea to follow a few simple rules when you have a cell phone. These rules will keep you out of trouble.

✗ I will not give out information about myself on the phone.

✗ I will not respond to messages that are mean or make me feel nervous.

✗ I will not post photos or videos of other people without asking them first.

✗ I will not share my passwords with anyone except my parents.

✔ I will use my phone only when I am allowed.

✔ If I see someone use his or her phone dangerously, I will tell an adult.

✔ I will ask my parents before I download a new app.

✔ I will keep my phone in a safe place like my backpack or my pocket.

Stay Connected

Talk to your parents or grandparents about their lives before cell phones existed. Chances are that they will tell you that cell phones have made their lives a lot easier. Before, people needed to use paper maps to get to new places. These maps were hard to read. Now, a cell phone can give them exact directions! Grown-ups can quickly bank or shop on their phones, too. Gone are the days of waiting in line.

Don't forget that the tiny computer in your hand is a telephone! Use it to talk to people. It is important to stay in touch with your family and friends. Cell phones can be your connection to the world!

Popular Pokémon

In 2016, Pokémon GO® became one of the most popular cell phone games of all time. It lets players explore the world and catch more than 100 Pokémon® characters.

Blinged-Out Phone!

People can go overboard with a new phone. One jeweler sold a diamond rose iPhone 4 that he decorated with real gold and diamonds. It cost around $8 million.

Glossary

addiction—an unhealthy behavior that is hard to stop

capabilities—things that something can do

components—parts of a system

defective—having flaws

disinfect—to clean something by killing germs

downloaded—copied a file from the Internet

fragile—easily broken

icons—small images on a device's screen with an app logo on them

livestock—farm animals

opinions—views or ideas about something

panic—sudden, strong fear

phobia—an extreme fear of something

privilege—a special right that not everyone has

recalled—asked people to return a product because of a problem

Index

Check It Out!

Books

Bright, Bonnie. 2013. *Cellphoneitus*. Create Space Independent Publishing Platform.

Cook, Julia. 2012. *Cell Phoney*. National Center for Youth Issues.

Enz, Tammy. 2013. *The Amazing Story of Cell Phone Technology*. Capstone Press.

Videos

Amaya's Story—Using Cell Phones Wisely. www.commonsensemedia.org/videos/amayas -story-using-cell-phones-wisely.

TED Talks. *How Mobile Phones Can Fight Poverty*. www.ted.com/talks/iqbal_quadir_says _mobiles_fight_poverty.

Websites

Safe Kids. *10 Rules for Safe Family Cell Phone Use*. www.safekids.com/rules-for-family-cell -phone-use/.

Today I Found Out. *15 Fascinating Cell Phone- Related Facts You Probably Didn't Know*. www.todayifoundout.com.

Try It!

In 2016, when Natalie Hampton was 16, she created Sit With Us, an app that helps students find others to sit with at lunch. Natalie had been bullied in school and didn't want others to suffer the way she had.

If you could create an app, what problem would you want to solve?

- What would you name your app?

- How would it work?

- Share your app idea with a few friends.

- Use their feedback to improve your idea.

About the Author

Lesley Ward is an author and a former children's magazine editor. Now, she lives in the heart of Kentucky. She shares her farm with a lot of horses, cats, and dogs. She uses her cell phone to send lots of texts to family and friends. She also uses her phone to take cute pictures of all of her animals.

Characters with Courage

Ben Nussbaum

Publishing Credits

Rachelle Cracchiolo, M.S.Ed., *Publisher*
Conni Medina, M.A.Ed., *Managing Editor*
Nika Fabienke, Ed.D., *Series Developer*
June Kikuchi, *Content Director*
John Leach, *Assistant Editor*
Lee Aucoin, *Senior Graphic Designer*

TIME For Kids and the TIME For Kids logo are registered trademarks of TIME Inc. Used under license.

Image Credits: p.5 (inset) Reuters TV/Reuters/Newscom; pp.10–11, p.12 (pilot) Xinhua/Alamy Stock Photo; p.12 Alamy Stock Photo; pp.12–13 Marka/Alamy Stock Photo; p.14 Ben Gabbe/WireImage/Getty Images; pp.16–17 United Archives GmbH/Alamy Stock Photo; p.18 Pictorial Press Ltd/Alamy Stock Photo; p.20 Mary Evans Picture Library/Alamy Stock Photo; pp.22–23 Universal Pictures/Getty Images; pp.24–25 PJF Military Collection/Alamy Stock Photo; p.25 Illustration by Timothy J. Bradley; pp.26–27 Rolls Press/Popperfoto/Getty Images; all other images from iStock and/or Shutterstock.

Teacher Created Materials

5301 Oceanus Drive
Huntington Beach, CA 92649-1030
http://www.tcmpub.com

ISBN 978-1-4258-4980-1

© 2018 Teacher Created Materials, Inc.
Printed in Malaysia
Thumbprints.042019

Table of Contents

Life or Death

A family is stranded on an island. They have nothing to eat or drink. An astronaut battles an alien. A plane crashes. A few survivors wander in the wild. These fictional characters are in danger. They are fighting to survive. It is life or death.

Sometimes when people arc under pressure, they show their true selves. That is one reason survival books are popular. They communicate special messages. They show how a character's best traits shine through when times are tough.

Books about survival are exciting to read. They can also be inspiring. The same things that help characters when they are desperate can help real people in day-to-day life.

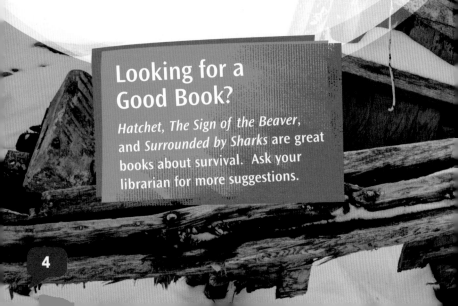

Looking for a Good Book?

Hatchet, The Sign of the Beaver, and Surrounded by Sharks are great books about survival. Ask your librarian for more suggestions.

Real-Life Survival

In 2010, three teens survived being stuck on a small boat in the Pacific Ocean. They were lost for 50 days. They drank water from rain collected in a tarp. They had food only when waves brought small fish into the boat.

A Resourceful Rider

    The Black Stallion, by Walter Farley, is a true classic. The book starts with a bang. A boy named Alec Ramsay is on a ship that is sinking in a storm. A wild horse is tied up in one of the ship's rooms and will drown if Alec does not help. Even though Alec is afraid that the fierce animal might kick him, he unties it. Seconds later, they plunge into the water together.

A Racer

The Black Stallion is an Arabian horse. This breed is known for its speed and **endurance**. In the book, Farley describes the horse's speed. He wrote, "like a shot from a gun, the Black broke down the beach. ...His huge strides seemed to make him fly through the air."

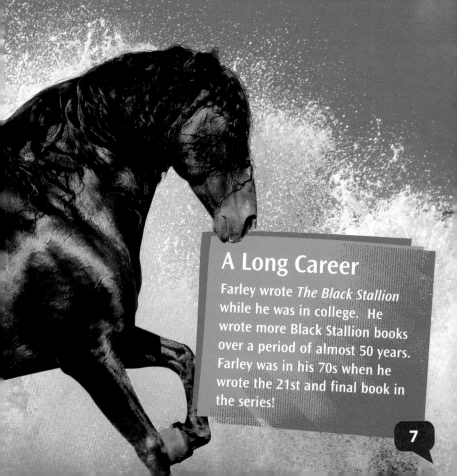

The boy and the horse swim for hours. The horse's instincts guide it to a small, uninhabited island. But Alec and the stallion are not safe. There is little food and no shelter. Working together, they survive until they are rescued. Back home, the stallion becomes a great racehorse.

A Long Career

Farley wrote *The Black Stallion* while he was in college. He wrote more Black Stallion books over a period of almost 50 years. Farley was in his 70s when he wrote the 21st and final book in the series!

Alec is tough, brave, and **self-reliant**. But more than anything, he is **resourceful** in the face of fear. This quality is the key to his survival. Resourceful people figure out how to do things. They experiment and **improvise**.

Alec's can-do attitude is communicated through his actions. He figures out how to start a fire by rubbing sticks together. He does not have the best tools, but he makes do with what he can find.

Sometimes, being resourceful means failing and then trying again. For example, Alec figures out a way to fish through trial and error. He uses bark to tie his pocketknife to a long stick. This spear does not work right away. He spends all day teaching himself how to use it.

The Stories Continue

Walter Farley's son Steven has continued writing the Black Stallion series. Steven's first book was *The Young Black Stallion*. He wrote the book with his father.

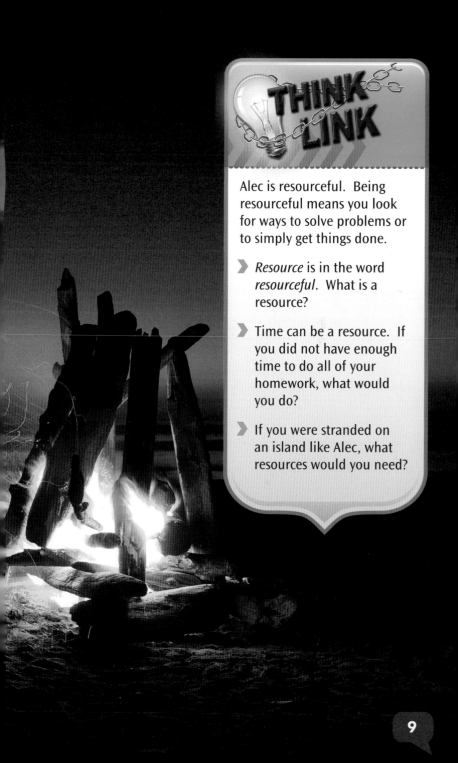

THINK LINK

Alec is resourceful. Being resourceful means you look for ways to solve problems or to simply get things done.

❯ *Resource* is in the word *resourceful*. What is a resource?

❯ Time can be a resource. If you did not have enough time to do all of your homework, what would you do?

❯ If you were stranded on an island like Alec, what resources would you need?

A young woman takes her father's place in the emperor's army. She pretends to be a man because the army is for men only. And she ends up becoming a great warrior. The emperor rewards her. She returns to her family.

If that sounds familiar, you have probably seen Disney's *Mulan*. The story is based on a short, very old Chinese poem. In the poem, Mulan spends 12 years as a soldier. "She goes ten thousand miles on the business of war," it says. The war is fierce. "Generals die in a hundred battles."

Mulan has a special place in Chinese culture. The legend of Mulan began in a poem. Plays, operas, art, novels, TV shows, and movies have all added details to the tale.

Flower Power

In Chinese, *mulan* is a type of flowering tree. Mulan's family name is *Hua*, which means *flower*.

opera of Mulan at a theater in China

Screen Star

Mulan Joins the Army was released in Shanghai, China, in 1939. The film became a smash hit. It launched many other movies and TV shows about Mulan.

Mulan loves her family. She is fierce and brave. But what really makes her special is her creativity. She does not do the same thing as everyone else. She has unique ideas.

One theme is the same in all Mulan stories: expect the unexpected. In the Disney movie, the enemy attacks Mulan and her fellow soldiers. Her friends are ready to die with honor. But Mulan finds a solution. She uses a cannon to start an **avalanche**. It buries the enemy army in the snow.

Women Warriors

Today, women are able to fight in the military in China. Women have been trained to fly fighter jets. A new all-woman **honor guard** has been featured at major events.

"Wei" Cool

In Mulan's time, China was a group of kingdoms instead of one country. Her story is set in the Wei dynasty in the north. This dynasty is famous for its beautiful art.

Mulan the Musical in New York City

A Singing Ballad

The first poem about Mulan uses a special style of poetry called *yuefu* (YWEH-foo). These poems were usually sung to music during special events. The music for these poems was lost, but the poems themselves survived.

Mulan is creative and decisive. Once she makes up her mind, she acts right away. When she has the idea to take her father's place in the military, she moves quickly. She does not hesitate.

Being too decisive is not always good. Sometimes, it is better to listen to what people think before you make a decision. But in the army, acting quickly is sometimes the only way to survive.

In one story, Mulan notices birds above the enemy camp at night. She realizes that this means the enemy soldiers are on the move. There is no time to wait. She orders her troops to prepare an attack. The enemy army is destroyed.

Real Mulans

By one estimate, 400 women fought as men in the American Civil War. The uniforms did not fit very well, and the armies were loosely organized. It was easy to join with a fake name.

Magical Friends

Imagine being thrown into a world of magic. You have no family. And you are in grave danger! J. K. Rowling's Harry Potter book series is about a young wizard. He must fight against the evil wizard Voldemort.

Harry is brave, skilled, and sometimes lucky. But he could never survive alone. He gets help from his friends, especially his best friends, Ron and Hermione. Even in a showdown with Voldemort, Harry thinks about his friends. In the fifth movie, he tells the dark lord, "You're the one who is weak. You will never know love or friendship."

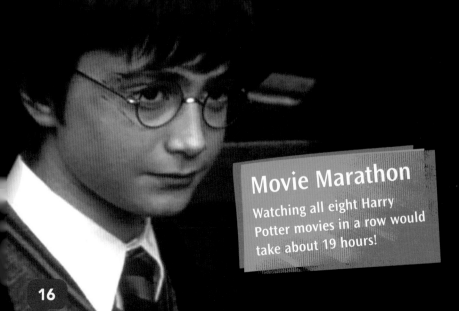

Movie Marathon

Watching all eight Harry Potter movies in a row would take about 19 hours!

Across Generations

Harry's father was friends with Sirius Black and Remus Lupin. Both of these men look after Harry throughout the series. This is another way that J. K. Rowling shows the power of friendship.

Hermione and Ron help Harry in many ways. In the first book, the friends must overcome seven challenges to get to a powerful object called the *sorcerer's stone.*

Hermione leads the team through a large, magical plant called *devil's snare.* Ron makes sure Harry and Hermione get to the other side of a life-size game of wizard's chess. In another challenge, Hermione figures out which potion is safe to drink. Without his friends, Harry would not have made it past these obstacles.

The lesson J. K. Rowling communicates with these characters is simple but important: to have friends, you have to be a friend. Harry cares for others. This does not make him weak. It is the way he survives.

STOP! THINK...

The movie based on the first book in the series, *Harry Potter and the Sorcerer's Stone*, was a hit around the world. This bar graph shows how much money it made in the United States, Japan, and some countries in Europe. Do you think the theme of the importance of friendship would be valued all over the world?

> What do these numbers show about the movie's popularity?

> Why would some movies be more popular in certain countries?

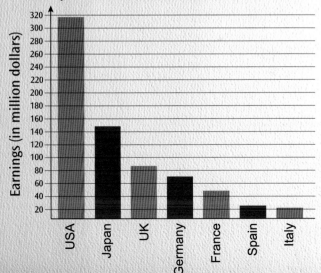

Earnings by Country of
Harry Potter and the Sorcerer's Stone

Earnings (in million dollars)

USA · Japan · UK · Germany · France · Spain · Italy

The Island Girl

Island of the Blue Dolphins, by Scott O'Dell, is about Karana. She is 12 years old at the start of the book. Her tribe lives on a small island. Hunters come to the island to gather otter **pelts**. In a fight between Karana's people and the hunters, many people in her tribe die.

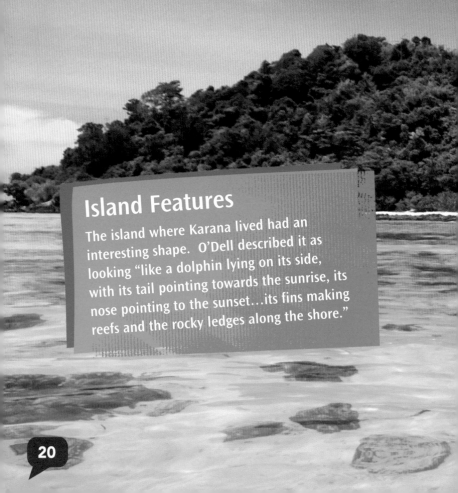

Island Features

The island where Karana lived had an interesting shape. O'Dell described it as looking "like a dolphin lying on its side, with its tail pointing towards the sunrise, its nose pointing to the sunset...its fins making reefs and the rocky ledges along the shore."

Later, a ship arrives to take Karana's tribe to the mainland. Spanish priests think the tribespeople will be safer there. As the ship departs, Karana spots her brother running toward it. She dives into the water and swims to him. Karana and her brother watch the ship sail away.

Just a few days later, wild dogs kill her brother. Karana is alone and afraid.

Island Connection

O'Dell, the author of *Island of the Blue Dolphins*, lived on Rattlesnake Island when he was a child. Today, it is called Terminal Island. It is part of Los Angeles.

Karana builds a life for herself. She makes a home and **tames** a wild dog. She even keeps two birds as pets.

Karana is **resilient**. She moves on from sadness and disappointment. She does not stay upset. Resilience is related to **optimism**. To be resilient, you have to look to the future instead of dwelling on the past.

One day, Karana tries to leave the island. But she has to return when her canoe leaks. It becomes too dangerous. She realizes she can't leave the island without help. She is also exhausted. After she sleeps for a day, she immediately sets to work making a better shelter. This is resilience in action!

Family Ties

Zia, the sequel to *Island of the Blue Dolphins*, is about Karana's niece, Zia. She lives in a **mission** on the mainland. She never gives up hope that her aunt will be rescued from the island.

Karana (right) in the 1964 *Island of the Blue Dolphins* film

Be Kind

Is there a connection between being resilient and being kind? Researchers think so. Being kind can actually make you more resilient!

The Real Karana

Karana is based on a real person. A woman lived alone on San Nicolas Island. This small island is about 60 miles from the coast of California. She was there for 18 years before she was rescued.

No one knows what her birth name was. She was taken to the mainland in 1853 and died seven weeks later. Priests called her Juana Maria. Today, some people call her the Lone Woman of San Nicolas.

Juana Maria made water bottles out of sea grass and asphaltum, a tar-like substance that washed ashore. The island has many freshwater springs, particularly on the western side.

She sometimes camped out in simple huts around the island to be near sources of food. She was discovered here, near a hut made of whale ribs and sealskin.

Juana Maria lived in a long, narrow cave. It kept out the fierce winds from the Pacific Ocean.

The woman ate a variety of food, including dried seal fat. This required heavy chewing and wore down her teeth. She killed seals at night, using stone weapons.

George Nidever led the expedition that brought the lone woman to the mainland. He said, "She must have been about 50 years old but was still strong and active. Her face was pleasing, as she was continuously smiling."

Researchers think this is the location of the last occupied native village on the island.

The island's highest elevation is 905 feet.

In 1933, the U.S. Navy took over the island. Today, there is an airplane runway on its east side.

Juana Maria

Everyday Survival

Few people have to face survival situations like the characters in these stories, but normal life has plenty of obstacles. Pressure and stress are everywhere.

Imagine that you do not have electricity for a few days after a huge storm. How could you be resourceful to find ways to keep warm? Imagine that you move to a new school. How could you make new friends? It would help to be resilient.

Hard things happen every day! This means each day you have a chance to communicate what is special about you. Survival skills can come in handy in many situations.

Be Prepared

Does your family have an emergency kit at home and in your car? *Ready.gov* has tips for what to put in the kit.

At the Movies

Actor Tom Hanks plays an astronaut in the movie *Apollo 13*. He and two other men go on a mission to the moon, but something goes wrong. The film was a huge hit when it was released in 1995.

Glossary

avalanche—a large amount of snow sliding down a mountain

culture—the habits, behaviors, and beliefs of a people, place, or time

endurance—the ability to put up with strain or suffering

honor guard—a military group used for ceremonies and other special occasions

improvise—to act without a plan

mission—the home, church, and community of a group of Christian people

operas—plays where the words are sung and an orchestra plays the music

optimism—the quality of expecting good things and looking at the positive parts of a situation

pelts—the skin and fur of animals

resilient—tending to recover from bad events

resourceful—able to figure out solutions without having a plan or tools

self-reliant—able to take care of oneself

showdown—a fight that will settle a disagreement

tames—makes gentle

uninhabited—without any people living there

Index

Check It Out!

Books

Farley, Walter. 1941. *The Black Stallion*. Yearling Classics.

Northrop, Michael. 2014. *Surrounded by Sharks*. Scholastic.

O'Dell, Scott. 1960. *Island of the Blue Dolphins*. Houghton Mifflin.

Paulsen, Gary. 1999. *Hatchet*. Simon & Schuster.

Rowling, J. K. 1997. *Harry Potter and the Sorcerer's Stone*. Scholastic.

Speare, Elizabeth George. 1983. *The Sign of the Beaver*. Houghton Mifflin.

Videos

Borsos, Phillip. 1995. *Far from Home: The Adventures of Yellow Dog*.

Cook, Barry, and Tony Bancroft. 1998. *Mulan*. Walt Disney Pictures.

Howard, Ron. 1995. *Apollo 13*.

Websites

Department of Homeland Security. *Ready*. www.ready.gov.

Rowling, J. K. Pottermore. www.pottermore.com.

Try It!

Being stuck on an island is a classic survival situation. It has been used in countless books, movies, and TV shows. What would you do if you were stranded on an island?

- ✖ Write a short survival story. Create a fictional character based on yourself.

- ✖ In what ways will you show readers your survival skills and traits?

- ✖ Describe how you feel. Are you afraid? Are you calm?

- ✖ Draw a map of the island. Label important locations and features.

Deserted Island

About the Author

Ben Nussbaum lives with his wife, two kids, a cat, and a red betta fish. He has written dozens of books for children. He has worked at *USA Today* and with Disney. He is now a freelance writer and editor based in Arlington, Virginia.

His favorite Black Stallion book is *The Island Stallion*. Some of his favorite nonfiction survival stories are *Into Thin Air*, *Endurance*, and *The Perfect Storm*.

Showdown

The Fight for Space

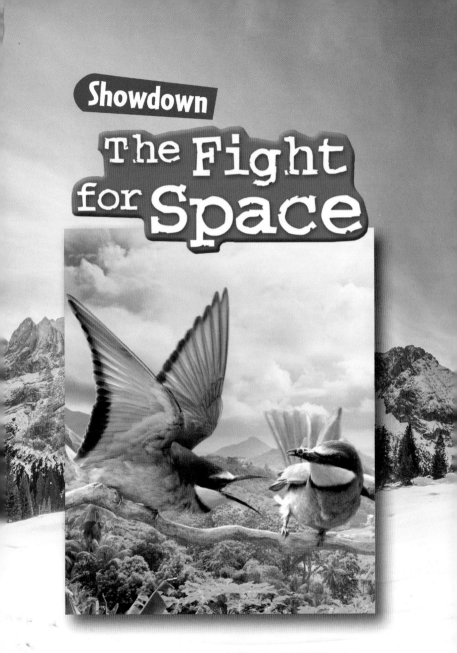

Dona Herweck Rice

Consultant

William B. Rice
Engineering Geologist

Publishing Credits

Rachelle Cracchiolo, *M.S.Ed., Publisher*
Conni Medina, M.A.Ed., *Managing Editor*
Nika Fabienke, Ed.D., *Series Developer*
June Kikuchi, *Content Director*
Seth Rogers, *Editor*
Michelle Jovin, M.A., *Assistant Editor*
Kevin Pham, *Graphic Designer*

TIME For Kids and the TIME For Kids logo are registered trademarks of TIME Inc. Used under license.

Image Credits: p.11 (inset) Andrey Nekrasov/Alamy Stock Photo; p.12 (inset) age fotostock/Alamy Stock Photo; pp.16-17 Nature Picture Library/Alamy Stock Photo; pp.22-23 Illustrations by Timothy J. Bradley; p.30 (inset) Rosanne Tackaberry/Alamy Stock Photo; pp.36-37 Jeffrey L. Rotman/Getty Images; all other images from iStock and/or Shutterstock.

Library of Congress Cataloging-in-Publication Data

Names: Rice, Dona, author.
Title: Showdown : the fight for space / Dona Herweck Rice.
Description: Huntington Beach, CA : Teacher Created Materials, [2018] | Audience: Grade 4 to 6. | Includes index.
Identifiers: LCCN 2017023528 (print) | LCCN 2017030010 (ebook) | ISBN 9781425854676 (eBook) | ISBN 9781425849917 (pbk.)
Subjects: LCSH: Animal behavior--Juvenile literature. | Animals--Habitations--Juvenile literature.
Classification: LCC QL751.5 (ebook) | LCC QL751.5 .R55 2018 (print) | DDC 591.5--dc23
LC record available at https://lccn.loc.gov/2017023528

Teacher Created Materials
5301 Oceanus Drive
Huntington Beach, CA 92649-1030
http://www.tcmpub.com
ISBN 978-1-4258-4991-7
© 2018 Teacher Created Materials, Inc.
Made in China
Nordica.092017.CA21701119

Table of Contents

There Once Was a Town

There once was a young town in the low, green hills of the West. People moved there from the big cities and areas already heavy with population. They wanted to live among the open hillsides and old farmlands. They liked the wild, natural spaces that still existed amid the new homes and businesses. The people who were not used to the natural world at their doorsteps thought they had found a paradise. In many ways, they had.

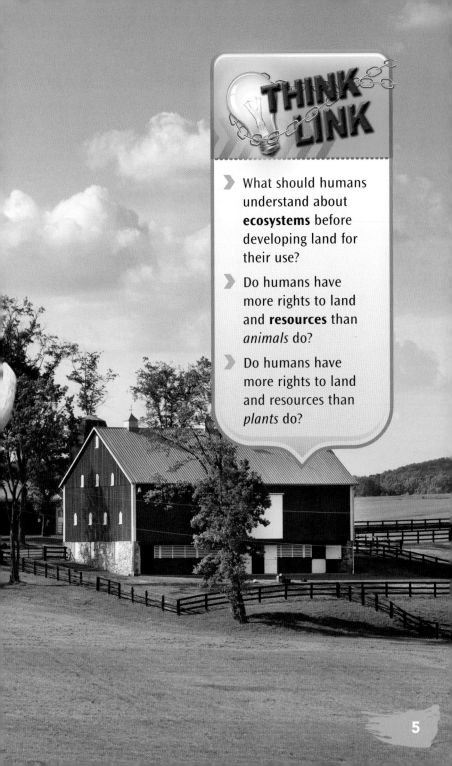

> What should humans understand about **ecosystems** before developing land for their use?

> Do humans have more rights to land and **resources** than *animals* do?

> Do humans have more rights to land and resources than *plants* do?

Life seemed perfect for the people in the town. There was just one problem. Others already lived on the land. Animals large and small had made this place their home for many years, and they had nowhere else to go. Looking for open land and resources, the animals shared the humans' new space.

Coyotes hunted as they always did, but their **prey** now included the small pets of the families living there. Snakes sometimes coiled in backyards under hoses and barbecue grills, looking for shelter and warmth. And in the dark of night, mice, possums, and skunks wandered free and enjoyed the fruits of family gardens.

Pet Protection

In areas where people live close to nature, they must protect their pets. Foxes and other animals that hunt find their next meals wherever they can. Small dogs and cats left unattended can become prey.

Spiders: Friends or Foes?

Living closely with nature means living with spiders—and that's a good thing! Spiders help maintain the population of insects. But some spiders are dangerous to humans. A harmful black widow might be found in a backyard wood stack as easily as a harmless jumping spider hiding behind curtains.

Relationships Among Species

It is important to understand what happens when different species **vie** for the same resources. To do this, you must first understand the ways species interact. Every species is, at any given time, doing its best to survive. Each species lives by **instinct** and nature. These things work together to keep the species alive and healthy. The instinct to survive is strong.

Most species do not make a plan for living side by side with other species. Only humans can do that. Whether humans actually make a plan is another story.

Growth and Changes

Growth and changes in a species is impacted most by changes in their environment. Changes in **habitat** and climate play a role, too. So do the ways in which species interact with each other. These changes can affect entire ecosystems.

Community

When two or more species interact in a given place, it is known as an *ecological community*. What one species does affects the other. Species in the same place do not exist apart from one another. Instead, they depend on each other to survive.

There are four basic relationships that species can have. Each type has to do with the way in which species interact. The relationships are mutualism, commensalism, predation, and competition.

Mutualism

Mutualism is when both sides benefit. Each side gives, and each side receives. Neither is harmed; both are helped.

Bees and flowers practice mutualism. Bees gather nectar from flowers. The nectar becomes their food. Bees also carry pollen from flower to flower. In this way, they assist the flowers' **reproduction**. The existence of each depends on the other.

Unlikely Friendship

The oxpecker is a type of bird whose name gives some indication as to what it does. It lands on zebras (and oxen, too) and picks insects from their hides. In this example of mutualism, the bird gets food and the zebra is saved from annoyance and parasites.

Spider crabs and algae have a mutualistic relationship. Look at the photo in the circle. You can see algae living on a crab's back. This helps the crab blend in and gives the algae a place to live. Think about what you see, and consider these questions:

> What would happen to the crab if there were no algae? What would happen to the algae if there was no crab?

> Does either partner benefit more than the other?

11

Commensalism

A relationship between two species in which one benefits and the other is neither helped nor harmed is known as *commensalism*. It can be found in many places in nature. Monarch butterflies and milkweeds are a good example.

Colorful monarchs catch the eye of **predators**. But predators avoid monarchs. They know that these butterflies taste bad. Monarchs feed on milkweed. A **toxin** in the plant is harmful to many vertebrates. Monarchs are not harmed by it, and they store it in their body. The act of the monarch storing the toxin benefits the butterfly, but it does not help or hurt the milkweed.

Dinner on the Go

As herds of cattle move about grassy fields, they stir up insects. The cattle and their waste also draw insects. All of that is good news for cattle egrets. They follow the herds and eat the readily available insects as they go. This does not hurt or help the cattle, but it is a big win for the egrets!

Can I Get a Ride?

Emperor shrimp are easy prey because they move so slowly. They catch rides on passing sea cucumbers. In this way, they can easily get from food source to food source without any trouble, and they are protected as they go. Sea cucumbers barely notice their presence.

Predation

Predation is the relationship of predators and prey. One animal lives, and the other dies. Prey do not benefit in predation, but an ecosystem may. Predators keep prey from becoming too **populous**. Too many of one species is not good and can hurt other species.

For example, rabbits reproduce quickly and in big numbers. They can overrun the plant life if their numbers are not kept in check. Predators, such as wolves, eat rabbits. They keep rabbit numbers down. This helps keep the ecosystem in balance.

We Are What We Eat

All animals can be classified into three types of **consumers.** Some animals are herbivores. That means they only eat plants. Sheep, deer, and cows are all herbivores. Meat eaters are carnivores. Lions and sharks are carnivores. Animals that eat both plants and animals are omnivores. Pigs and bears are omnivores.

Parasitism

When a predator feeds off a living host, the predator is called a *parasite*. In this relationship, the parasite is benefited and the host is harmed. A mosquito is a parasite. When it bites a human, a small, red bump appears. The bump is the place where the mosquito drank the human's blood.

Competition

The most harmful relationship to the health of an ecosystem may be *competition*. Neither species benefits from this relationship. Both are harmed.

Each species has a **niche** in nature. But species compete when resources are scarce. This may be due to natural causes, such as fires or floods. It may also happen through human involvement, such as when trees are cut to build homes.

Both species need the resource, and they fight for it. One species wins and takes ownership of the resource. The other species may die out. While mutual, commensal, and predatory relationships help keep an ecosystem balanced, competition does not.

Cheetahs vs. Lions

All species compete for resources. Sometimes, they compete with other members of their own species. Sometimes, they compete with members of a different species. Cheetahs and lions are old competitors. They eat the same kind of prey and will compete to eat. If a lion sees a cheetah with food, the lion may attack the cheetah.

Biotic and Abiotic

All things in an ecosystem are either *biotic* or *abiotic*. Biotic things are living. These can include plants and animals. Abiotic things are not living. These include water, soil, and sunlight.

Human Factor

If humans enter an ecosystem and take the resources that other living things need—such as land—competition begins. Most often, humans win. But scientists say the win is only for the short term. The damage done to the ecosystem creates an **imbalance** that has far-reaching effects.

Humans are part of a **dynamic** web of biotic and abiotic things. When one piece of the web is changed, everything is affected. The full effects may take time to see, but they cannot be avoided. Humans are an important part of the world, and they need resources, too. But balance is key.

Community Ecology

Community ecologists watch how species in an ecosystem interact. They look at what role each species plays. They also track changes in biotic lives.

A Niche for One

No two species can exist in the same niche for a long period of time. The species will fight for the resources there. One of the species will eventually become extinct.

Natural Selection

Each living species is made of **traits** found in its **DNA**. Those qualities determine all aspects of how a species looks and its instincts. Over time, traits change as they **adapt** to the species' environment.

The traits that help the species thrive are the ones that survive into future generations. When these traits are passed onto offspring, it is known as *heredity*. This is nature's way of selecting healthy traits that do well in the world. That is why this process is called *natural selection*.

Artificial Selection

Animal breeders often pick traits that they want to pass on in a species. For example, a breeder might want a dog that walks a certain way or has a long coat. This is known as *artificial selection*.

Heredity

Heredity is the process by which traits are passed to offspring. For instance, the color of your hair, your eyes, and your skin are all traits. These, along with many more traits, are passed down to you from your **biological** parents through heredity.

21

Survival of the Fittest

Organisms and traits that are most suited for an environment are the ones that survive. Organisms reproduce and their traits are passed on to future generations. This is what is meant by "survival of the fittest."

The drawings below depict survival of the fittest. The phrase was first used to explain trait adaptations. Understanding survival of the fittest is key to understanding competition among species. It is through adaptation that the fit survive.

At first, there is enough food for everybody.

2 As more animals eat the food, the easiest to reach food gets used up. The smallest animals can't reach the food that is left, and die off.

3 After a while, the only food left is in the hardest to reach places. Only animals that can reach this food survive.

4 In the end, the only animals left are the ones that can still get to the food source.

23

Showdown: Inside Habitats

Who would win in a habitat that is shared by both humans and animals? The first step in predicting a winner is to explore the relationships among species. Then, look at other habitats to see how those relationships play out. Think about what happens in habitats as humans compete for resources. Humans always have an impact. More than that, humans are the only species who can figure out how to make a system work for other species.

No other species can predict the impact of its choices the way humans can. In fact, most species cannot make choices at all. Humans have that freedom. And with freedom comes responsibility.

Moral Monkeys

Many scientists study animals to see if they can make **moral** choices. One study was done on a group of monkeys that learned to push a lever to get food. Later on, the monkeys learned that when they pushed the lever, another monkey would get an electric shock. After that, the monkeys refused to push the lever— even if they were very hungry.

Empathetic Elephants

Some people wonder if animals other than humans have empathy. Empathy is the ability to feel what another person or thing feels. One story about elephants says that an old woman with poor eyesight got lost in a jungle. Elephants covered her with branches to keep her safe. They also stood guard until help came.

Chaparral

A chaparral is a habitat in which cool ocean air meets a hot landmass. The area may be flat, hilly, or mountainous. It is often very hot and dry for about half the year. The rest of the year is wet. The long, dry period may result in wildfires.

A chaparral's climate is appealing to many living things. This habitat is common in California, where coastal land is costly to own. Many people move to chaparrals, where land is more affordable and the weather is still pleasant. But as more and more people move there, they create problems.

Space Invaders

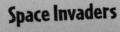

During much of the year, days can be hot in chaparrals. Many of the animals there are nocturnal. They sleep during the hottest part of the day and roam at night. The areas around people's houses in chaparrals may be overrun with lizards, rabbits, chipmunks, and more. Each species finds food wherever it can. Often, this means invading human space.

Water Blues

Animals and plants in chaparrals must live with little water. This is one of the biggest challenges of life in chaparrals. People tend to use most of the water. That makes life harder for the other species in the habitat.

Not so long ago, many chaparrals were just open land. Then, animals became **displaced** as people developed this land.

Now, human interactions disturb the wildlife in the area. People bring in non-native plants. They grow lawns and keep flowering plants that use more water than the area has. People try to maintain ways of life that they enjoyed in different habitats. The result is an overuse of resources. It causes displacement of species as their land is overrun. They have nowhere else to go. The animals and humans vie for the same space and resources. There is not enough for everyone. Some species will lose the battle.

Every Continent

Chaparrals can be found all over the world. The West Coast of the United States is home to many chaparral habitats. They can also be found in Chile, South Africa (pictured right), and Australia.

Pollution

As more people move into chaparrals, they bring pollution. Pollution is anything that makes land, water, or air unsafe to use. Even the smallest amount of pollution will harm the wildlife that live there.

Rain Forest

The world's rain forests are lush habitats filled with a variety of animal and plant life. **Precipitation** and **transpiration** are high there.

Rain forests benefit people in many ways. They provide much of the world's oxygen. They are also a source for many medicines. But over the years, many rain forests have been cut down. The trees are used for lumber, and the land is cleared for farming. In the process, animals lose their homes. Many species have become endangered, and some have become extinct. Experts think droughts that have begun in the area are a result of deforestation.

Efforts are being made to stop the heavy deforestation. But progress is slow, and forests continue to fall.

Goodbye, Forests

The World Wildlife Fund estimates that Earth loses up to 58,000 square miles (150,000 square kilometers) of forest each year. That's more than 1 square mile (2.59 square kilometers) every 10 minutes!

Animals at Risk

Around 8 out of 10 of the world's known species live in rain forests. Deforestation puts a high number of those animals at risk.

Carbon-Based Life

Every living thing is made in part of **carbon**, which is found in the land, sea, and sky. Humans and many animals breathe out a gas called **carbon dioxide** (1). Plants use this gas to make their food. In turn, plants release oxygen (2), which many animals (including humans) breathe.

As people use resources, the balance of carbon in the atmosphere and in ecosystems is affected (3). This changes the climate and, therefore, affects animals as well. In the short term, humans benefit. But in the long term, whole ecosystems are altered. Animals must adapt or die.

Causes of Climate Change

Rain forest plants help to balance gas levels in the atmosphere. As large areas of rain forest are cut down, gas levels shift and the planet warms up. This leads to **climate change**.

carbon dioxide

3

carbon dioxide

1

2

oxygen

Ocean

Most of Earth is covered by oceans. Humans are not ocean animals, but they rely on ocean resources. In particular, they use sea animals as food sources.

For many years, Atlantic cod was a major food source. Many fishers made their livings catching cod. The ocean was filled with cod, and they stayed high on the food chain. Cod fed freely on other fish and helped to maintain the balance of the ecosystem. Their enormous size made many **fisheries** wealthy. But the demand for cod almost completely destroyed the species.

World's Largest

The ocean is the world's largest **biome**. It covers about 70 percent of Earth's surface. There are over one million species of plants and animals that live in the ocean. Scientists predict that there are millions more species that have not yet been discovered.

Coral Reefs

The ocean is the most **diverse** biome on Earth. Many ocean species find homes in coral reefs. Some studies suggest that 1 out of 4 ocean animals rely on coral reefs for food and shelter.

Humans **depleted** cod through overfishing. It reached a point that the cod could not recover. They could not reproduce in numbers big enough to allow some cod to grow to their full size. Many young cod were being eaten. Consequently, cod shrank in size, and they lost their place in the food chain.

Many fisheries have since collapsed. People have lost their jobs. The cod are still adapting to a new niche, as is everything in the ecosystem—including humans.

Unemployed

The cod industry had grown over the years. Then, in the 1990s, it collapsed. In a single day, more than 40,000 fishers in Canada lost their jobs.

Apex Predator

The cod was once an *apex predator*, meaning it was at the top of the food chain. After it lost its position in the food chain, the population of its prey consequently exploded.

Grasslands

Grasslands are marked by fields of grasses. Limited rainfall keeps many trees from growing. Large groups of animals make grasslands their home. Today, the land is often used for farming.

In North America, bison roamed the grasslands for many years. They were a major food source for American Indians. When European settlers came to the land, they hunted the bison almost to extinction.

The newcomers also wiped out many American Indians. They took away their food source and their land. American Indian numbers decreased. Their lives were changed forever.

Rabbit Trouble

In 1859, about 25 rabbits were brought from England to Australia. At the time, there were no rabbits there. Since then, they have overtaken the land. They have changed ecosystems. Many plants and animals have become endangered through competing with rabbits for resources.

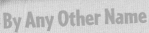

By Any Other Name

Grasslands are called *savannahs* in Africa. They are known as *rangelands* in Australia. Go to South America, and grasslands are called *llanos*. And in North America, grasslands are called *plains*.

All Connected

No species lives apart from others. The activity of every species has an effect on the whole ecosystem. And because ecosystems are connected, the whole planet is altered.

Competition is natural among some species. Life adapts. Some species get stronger. Others fall away. But sometimes, things happen beyond what is natural. Usually, these things happen at the hands of people. Humans often use more resources than they need. They may build and develop without care for other species and resources.

We know that what humans do affects not only other species but other humans, too. The impact may not be felt right away. But it *will* be felt, because all things in life are connected.

Constant Competition

Humans are in constant competition with small creatures. Some of these creatures use the same resources humans do. Flies, ants, and mosquitoes compete with humans for resources, such as space and food.

Butterfly Effect

The *butterfly effect* is a theory, which says that a small event in one place can have a huge impact somewhere else. The idea is that a butterfly might flap its wings and set off a chain reaction with massive results. Even a small event may have a big consequence.

Glossary

adapt—to change something to make it easier to live in an area

biological—used to describe parents who gave birth to a child

biome—a large community of plants and animals that live in a single place

carbon—a chemical element that is found in all living plants and animals

carbon dioxide—a colorless, odorless gas that is absorbed by plants to make food.

climate change—the recent increase in the world's temperature

consumers—organisms that feed on other organisms

depleted—used most or all of something

displaced—removed from the usual or proper place

diverse—made up of many different unlike elements

DNA—substance that carries a living thing's hereditary information

dynamic—always changing

ecosystems—all living and nonliving things in a particular environment

fisheries—businesses that catch and sell fish

habitat—the type of place where a plant or animal normally or naturally grows or lives

imbalance—a state in which things do not occur in equal or normal amounts

instinct—a way of behaving, feeling, or thinking that is natural and not learned

moral—concerned with what is right and wrong in human behavior

niche—an area where a species is best suited to survive

precipitation—water that falls to the ground as rain or snow

predators—animals that eat other animals as their food source

prey—animal that is hunted by other animals as their food source

reproduction—the process that results in new babies, animals, or plants

resources—things that provide something useful and necessary

toxin— a poison or venom of plant or animal origin

traits—characteristics that make one person or thing different from another

transpiration—the transfer of water from plants to the atmosphere

vie—to compete with others in an attempt to get something

Index

Check It Out!

Books

Burnie, David. 2011. *Eyewitness Plant*. DK Children.

Hopkinson, Deborah. 2005. *Who Was Charles Darwin?* Grosset & Dunlap.

National Geographic Kids. 2012. *125 True Stories of Amazing Animals*. National Geographic Children's Books.

Rice, William B. 2016. *Life and Non-Life in an Ecosystem*. Teacher Created Materials.

Rice, William B. 2016. *Life and the Flow of Energy*. Teacher Created Materials.

Videos

National Geographic Crittercam. www.animals. nationalgeographic.com/animals/crittercam/

Websites

BioExpedition. www.bioexpedition.com

National Geographic Kids. www.kids.nationalgeographic.com

World Wildlife Fund (WWF). www.worldwildlife.org

Try It!

You've just landed your dream job of working to protect animal habitats. But on your first day, there is already a huge problem! A company just bought a large piece of land where animals live, and they plan to turn the land into a shopping mall. It is up to you to save the animals!

🐾 Draw a picture of the land that is being bought. Make sure to label areas where animals live.

🐾 Try to determine if there is a way to share the land between the animals and the company. If so, draw your plan for the land. If not, think of ways to convince the company to build something that helps, not harms, the animals.

🐾 Write a letter to the company asking them to follow your plan. Be sure to include your drawing with your letter.

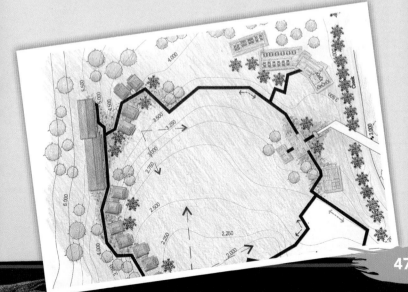

About the Author

Dona Herweck Rice has written hundreds of books, stories, and essays for kids on all kinds of topics, from pirates to why some people have bad breath! Writing is her passion. But she also loves reading, dancing, and singing at the top of her lungs (although she'd be the first to tell you that this is not really a pleasure for anyone else). Rice was a teacher and is an acting coach. She lives in Southern California with her husband, two sons, and a cute but very silly dog.

SLAM
Poetry

Elizabeth Siris Winchester

Consultants

Kenn Nesbitt
Children's Poet Laureate 2013–15

Publishing Credits

Rachelle Cracchiolo, M.S.Ed., *Publisher*
Conni Medina, M.A.Ed., *Managing Editor*
Nika Fabienke, Ed.D., *Series Developer*
June Kikuchi, *Content Director*
John Leach, *Assistant Editor*
Lee Aucoin, *Senior Graphic Designer*

Image Credits: Cover and p.1 Michael Loccisano/Getty Images for Mad Over You; Reader's Guide page Derek Davis/Portland Press Herald via Getty Images; pp.4, 5 Bennett Raglin/Getty Images for DreamYard Project; p.6 dpa picture alliance/Alamy Stock Photo; p.7 Christian K. Lee/The Washington Post via Getty Images; p.8 Patrick Farrell/Miami Herald/MCT via Getty Images; p.9 Tim Mosenfelder/Getty Images; p.13 Philip Scalia/Alamy Stock Photo; p.14 ZUMA Press, Inc./Alamy Stock Photo; pp.14–15 Jonathan Newton/The Washington Post via Getty Images; p.16 Dimitrios Kambouris/Getty Images for Tony Awards Productions; pp.16–17 Yoon S. Byun/The Boston Globe via Getty Images; pp.18–19, 21 Bennett Raglin/Getty Images for DreamYard Project; p.23 Michael Loccisano/Getty Images for Mad Over You; p.27 Patrick Farrell/Miami Herald/MCT via Getty Images; p.31 Barry Chin/The Boston Globe via Getty Images; all other images from iStock and/or Shutterstock.

Teacher Created Materials
5301 Oceanus Drive
Huntington Beach, CA 92649-1030
http://www.tcmpub.com
ISBN 978-1-4258-4981-8
© 2018 Teacher Created Materials, Inc.

Table of Contents

It's a Poetry Slam!

Slam poetry is a form of spoken word poetry. People write and perform it for others. But slam poets don't wear costumes or use **props** or music. Some poems have a **rhythmic** or musical sound when read aloud. Other poems don't.

Slam poets use words to express thoughts and make people feel something. Their words are powerful. Slam poetry is often about the author's identity, including his or her **race** or gender. Or it can be fun and silly.

There are rules for slam poetry competitions, known as *poetry slams*. But there are few rules for writing the actual poems. Slam poets write about anything. They use words as they wish and do not need to follow the usual grammar rules.

Students perform onstage at the Bronx-Wide Poetry Slam Finals.

4

About ME

Momma told me to know my story
She said, "Learn you and tell the world as you do"
To dream 3-point shots
but shoot to read everything
& give everything all you got
She warned about his stories found in schoolbooks given to me
Said be ready cause barely anyone in there will look like me
Think like me Like me
Then I found Poetry
Poetry like me
So I started writing
Started writing about me
About What I wanted to see
How I wanted to believe
In who I was to be
So I started writing to learn about me
ME

—½ Pint Poetics,
  Ravenswood
  Elementary School
  fifth graders,
  Chicago, Illinois

Write On!

People have always told stories. Poetry is one way to do so. A construction worker and poet named Marc Kelly Smith came up with a new way to share poetry with others. Smith started the poetry slam **movement**.

Smith felt that poets should be free to *not* follow rules. He thought poetry had lost its passion. In 1986, he started a weekly poetry reading. It was at a jazz club in Chicago, Illinois. His readings became popular. Smith hosted the first poetry slam at another Chicago jazz club. In poetry slams, judges from the audience score the poets. The scores are based on the writing and performance of the poetry.

Rhythmic Writers

Langston Hughes (LANG-stuhn HYOOZ) was an American poet. He wrote "jazz poetry." It had rhythms similar to the ones in blues and jazz music of the time.

Jordan Perry, 17, recites one of his poems in front of the Martin Luther King Jr. Memorial.

Slam poetry and poetry slams quickly spread across the United States. Slam poets shared their work in cafés and clubs. They read at open mic nights. These are events where inexperienced people perform for an audience. Anyone can go on stage to sing, tell jokes, perform poetry, and more. Slam poetry spread to other countries, too. Younger writers began to take part. In 1990, the first National Poetry Slam took place. It was held in San Francisco, California.

James Kass helped bring slam poetry to teens. He started the group Youth Speaks in 1996. Other groups teach slam poetry to elementary school kids.

That Rules!

Poetry slam rules can vary, but these are common:
- Poets compete as individuals or on teams.
- Poets must perform poems that they wrote themselves.
- Poets get three minutes to read one poem.
- Costumes, props, and instruments are not allowed.
- Judges are chosen from the audience. They give scores to the poets, which are used to figure out who competes in the next rounds and who wins.

James Kass (center) and Youth Speaks poets attend a premiere party for HBO's *Brave New Voices* and Youth Speaks in San Francisco, California.

TV Time

A television show that aired for five years also helped make slam poetry popular. It was called *Def Poetry Jam*. It allowed people to watch slam poets in action.

Earth Day

Trash on the ground ends up in the sea.
People use too much electricity.
Careless people leak oil into the sea
    like it was a dumpster.
All of this is starting to destroy her.
People pollute the air with their cars.
We don't want to end up like Mars.
People use way too much paper.
Global warming is making water into vapor.
Here's the problem: too much pollution.
Reduce, reuse, recycle is the solution.
We are like a **tsunami** washing away the earth.
Don't you think it hurts?
So these are some things we all can do
To stop making the earth feel blue.

1. Recycle more and throw out less trash.
2. Use less electricity by turning off the lights that
   are not in use.
3. Don't drive, instead bike or walk.
4. Use less paper cause it's wasting trees.

Make sure you do all of these.
Save the earth! Save the earth! Save the earth!
Don't be mean, be green!

—½ Pint Poetics, Lara Elementary
   Academy second graders,
   Chicago, Illinois

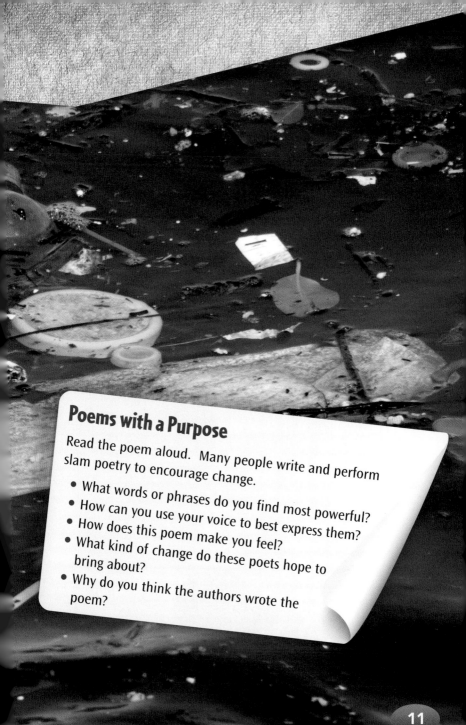

Poems with a Purpose

Read the poem aloud. Many people write and perform slam poetry to encourage change.

- What words or phrases do you find most powerful?
- How can you use your voice to best express them?
- How does this poem make you feel?
- What kind of change do these poets hope to bring about?
- Why do you think the authors wrote the poem?

Word Warriors

The Nuyorican (new-yo-REEK-in) Poets Cafe is in New York City. It opened in 1973. A group of Puerto Rican writers started it. The café is known for its open mic nights and Friday night poetry slams. Top poets compete in the Friday slams. People wait in lines to listen to slam poets.

Top performers can join the café's National Poetry Slam team. Groups from all over the United States compete in this event. People can compete in a group or perform **solo**. The café has other programs for poets, musicians, and actors of all ages.

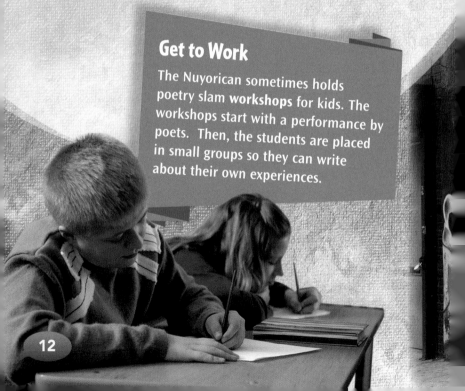

Get to Work

The Nuyorican sometimes holds poetry slam **workshops** for kids. The workshops start with a performance by poets. Then, the students are placed in small groups so they can write about their own experiences.

Poetry of the People

"Slam poetry events involve a lot of **interaction**," Daniel Gallant explains. He is the Nuyorican's executive director. "Slam poets rely on energy from the audience."

13

Poets in Chicago

Kuumba Lynx (KOOM-buh LIHNKS) is an urban arts youth group in Chicago. It was founded by Jaquanda Villegas (juh-KWAN-duh vee-YEY-guhs) and Jacinda Bullie (hah-SIHN-duh BUL-ee) more than 20 years ago. The group provides a safe place where teens can express their thoughts. In the group, teens connect with poetry through the use of hip-hop. Villegas says, "Like the **MC** in hip-hop, the slam poet has the power to move the crowd!"

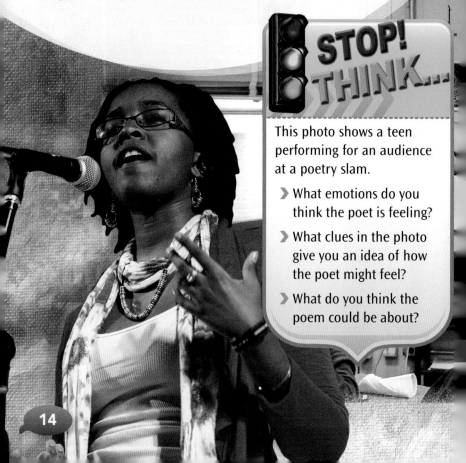

STOP! THINK...

This photo shows a teen performing for an audience at a poetry slam.

❯ What emotions do you think the poet is feeling?

❯ What clues in the photo give you an idea of how the poet might feel?

❯ What do you think the poem could be about?

In 2008, the group started a program for kids ages 8 to 14. It is called ½ Pint Poetics. Kids are taught to think and write about "class, race, gender, and global impact," says Bullie. School teams take part in a poetry slam each year. The slam ends with a hip-hop concert.

High school student Kyle Taylor hosts a regular poetry slam at his school.

Poets in San Francisco

Youth Speaks is based in San Francisco. It is for people ages 13 to 24. The group has programs across the country and around the world. It created the first national youth poetry slam in 1997. This event is called Brave New Voices. It takes place in a different U.S. city every year.

"We think every young person has a voice, and we want to work with youth to find their voice and present it," says Kass. "I started Youth Speaks to give young people a space to define who they are."

He Diggs It!

The hip-hop musical *Hamilton* is a Broadway smash hit. Daveed (dah-VEED) Diggs won a Tony Award® for playing the roles of Thomas Jefferson and the Marquis de Lafayette (mahr-KEE duh lah-fah-YEHT). He took part in Youth Speaks when he was in high school. He says poetry slams are the reason for his success.

Teens Talk

"I knew how much writing meant to me when I was young," Kass says. He suggests that kids watch slam poetry videos and see it live. "The most important thing is to be yourself and have fun."

You're a Poet, You Know It!

"Spoken word poetry is the art of performance poetry. It involves creating poetry that doesn't just want to sit on paper. Something about it demands it be heard out loud," says Sarah Kay.

Kay was in a poetry group in college with another student named Phil Kaye. Together, they started Project VOICE. The group teaches kids in all grades about spoken word poetry. The group has worked with hundreds of schools in over 20 countries.

Sarah writes poems to figure things out. Phil likes writing and sharing poems with others. Think about the words and meanings of this poem as you read it. Say it aloud, with feeling.

DreamYard Project hosted the Bronx-Wide Poetry Slam in 2016.

I have seen the best of you and the worst of
you and I choose both
I want to share every single one of your
sunshines and save some for later
I will tuck them into my pocket so I can give
them back to you when the rains fall hard
Friend
I want to be the mirror that reminds you to
love yourself
I want to be the air in your lungs that reminds
you to breathe easy
When the walls come down
When the thunder rumbles
When nobody else is home
Hold my hand
And I promise
I won't let go
—from "An Origin Story"
by Sarah Kay and Phil Kaye

Winner

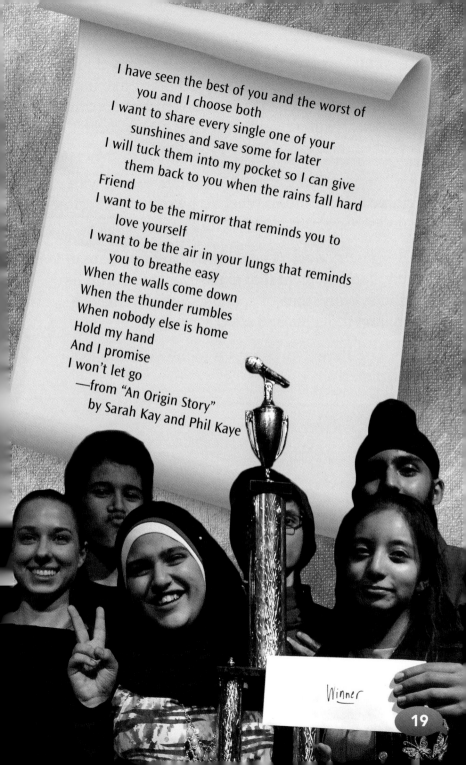

Phil Kaye found slam poetry in high school. "I thought poetry was something I didn't like until I saw someone…perform a spoken word poem," he says. "I still remember feeling, 'Wow! I can't believe this is something I'm allowed to do.'"

Project VOICE helps kids start writing with three big questions: What do I write about? How do I write about it? How do I perform it?

"Poetry doesn't necessarily have to be about a big, huge moment that makes you cry. It can be about a tiny thing," explains Kaye. "We have a million thoughts and ideas every day."

Use these two exercises to put your thoughts on paper!

Exercise 1: List It!

Make a list of three things you know to be true. The only rules are to use details and to not think too hard. For example, Kaye likes the Los Angeles Lakers, Friday afternoons, and chili. Kaye might say he likes chili because when he was little, his dad used to make it with him.

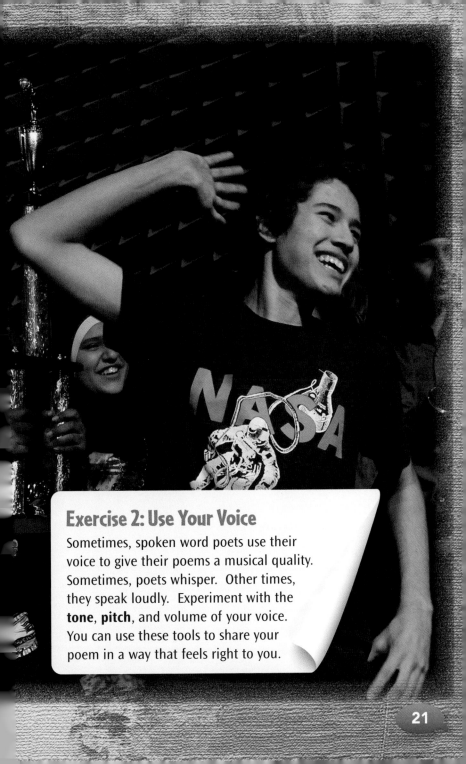

Exercise 2: Use Your Voice

Sometimes, spoken word poets use their voice to give their poems a musical quality. Sometimes, poets whisper. Other times, they speak loudly. Experiment with the **tone**, **pitch**, and volume of your voice. You can use these tools to share your poem in a way that feels right to you.

Poetry Rules!

There are three main categories of poetry. Lyric poems tell a person's thoughts or feelings. Narrative poetry tells a story. Dramatic poems use characters to act out a story. Each of these categories includes many forms of poems. Slam poetry is a form of lyric poetry.

When it comes to writing, slam poetry doesn't have any rules. But other types require poets to follow rules. For example, haiku has a certain number of syllables and lines. Other poems have rhyme patterns.

All poems are creative ways for people to express themselves. Rhythm is the way the language flows and sounds in a poem. Poetry often includes patterns known as *meter*.

Haiku

This Japanese poetry form has 17 syllables that are broken up into three lines. The first and third lines have five syllables. The second line has seven syllables. The poem often includes a word that tells or hints at the season the poet is writing about.

Fibonacci

These poems have six lines. Each line has a certain number of syllables. The order is 1, 1, 2, 3, 5, and 8 syllables.

Kids
Can
Create
Art like this.
Or make a new form
For themselves and for others, too.

How to Throw a Poetry Slam

½ Pint Poetics offers these tips for getting started:

🔊 Gather a crew of teachers, artists, students, and community members.

🔊 Get kids interested by having a slam poetry performance at a school assembly. Afterward, have students sign up to take part in a poetry slam.

🔊 Decide whether you will have a slam team or individual poets.

🔊 Classes could compete against each other, or school against school. Or kids could perform as individuals.

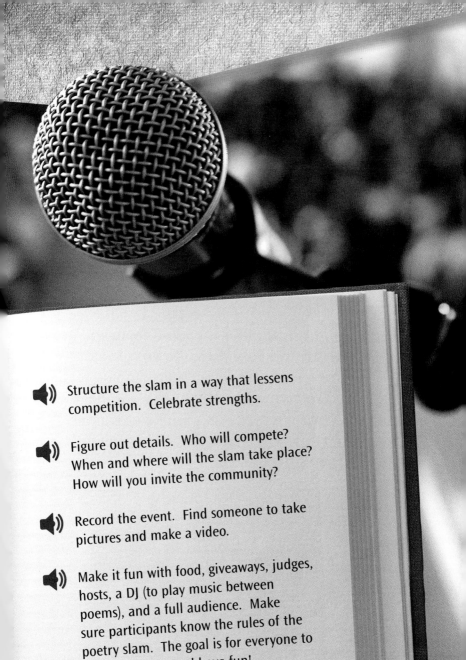

🔊 Structure the slam in a way that lessens competition. Celebrate strengths.

🔊 Figure out details. Who will compete? When and where will the slam take place? How will you invite the community?

🔊 Record the event. Find someone to take pictures and make a video.

🔊 Make it fun with food, giveaways, judges, hosts, a DJ (to play music between poems), and a full audience. Make sure participants know the rules of the poetry slam. The goal is for everyone to exchange ideas and have fun!

Find Your Voice

The sun rises. It's time to get out of bed.
Your mom rushing you along
    is something you dread.
Instead of getting angry, think about
    all there is to see and do
What exciting things might happen to you?
Write them down, you never know just
    where your thoughts might let you go!

Why not give slam poetry a try? Use the information throughout this book to help you get started. Remember that there are no rules for writing slam poetry. Find your voice and be real. "A writer is someone who thinks and has ideas about the world," says Jacinda Bullie of Kuumba Lynx. "We're all writers. Some just haven't put their thoughts on paper yet.

A Winning Writer

In 2012, Santino Panzica won the TFK Poetry Contest. Santino was only 12 when he won! The next year, he published his first book of poems. It is called *The Man-Eating Lemon*.

Contest Time

TIME For Kids holds an annual poetry contest. It is open to kids ages 8 to 13 in the United States. Kids can write and send in poems that are funny and rhyme. They must be original and not copy another poet's work.

Glossary

interaction—when people communicate or react to each other

MC—short for *master of ceremonies*; the person in charge of the microphone

movement—a series of acts working toward an end

pitch—a quality of sound that can be high or low

props—objects used by performers to create a certain effect

race—belonging to a group of people with the same ancestry

rhythmic—having a pattern of sounds or movements

solo—alone

tone—quality of spoken sound

tsunami—a large sea wave caused by an earthquake, volcano, or other changes underwater

workshops—educational meetings or discussions that allow people to learn about or explore a specific topic

Index

Check It Out!

Books

Regan, Dian Curtis. 2010. *Barnyard Slam*. Holiday House.

Swados, Elizabeth. 2002. *Hey You! C'mere! A Poetry Slam*. Arthur A. Levine Books.

Videos

LPS Media. *Wetherbee 3rd and 4th Grade Poetry Slam*.

Mali, Taylor. *On Girls Lending Pens*.

MentorTEAM. *Mentor Grade 6 Poetry Slam!*

Project VOICE. *An Origin Story*.

TED-Ed. *Miss Gayle's 5 Steps to Slam Poetry*.

THNKR. *Kioni "Popcorn" Marshall: Prodigy Poet*.

Websites

½ Pint Poetics. www.kuumbalynx.com/half-pint-poetics-2/.

Nuyorican Poets Cafe. www.nuyorican.org.

Project VOICE. www.projectvoice.co.

Youth Speaks. www.youthspeaks.org.

Try It!

Perform your poetry! Imagine that your school is hosting a poetry slam and needs kids to take part. You accept the challenge.

- 🔊 What will you write about?

- 🔊 Will your poem focus on a small moment or a big idea?

- 🔊 Use some of the tips in this book to get started. Share your poem with a friend.

- 🔊 Practice performing. Slam poets play with their voice to get their message across. You could whisper, yell, or even break into song.

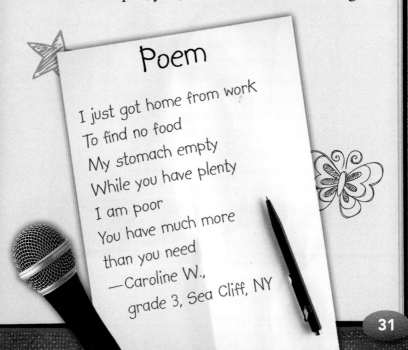

Poem

I just got home from work
To find no food
My stomach empty
While you have plenty
I am poor
You have much more
than you need
—Caroline W.,
grade 3, Sea Cliff, NY

About the Author

Elizabeth Siris Winchester has written for *TIME FOR KIDS* for almost 20 years. She has covered a range of topics from bullying, bats, and butterflies to amazing kids and groundbreaking figures. She is grateful to have found work that she enjoys and finds meaningful. She thanks her three kids for inspiring her often. She also loves running, yoga, baking, music, dogs, and especially time with friends and family.

Communicate!

Documentaries

Kelly Rodgers

Consultant

Laura Waters, M.A.
Professor of Communications

Publishing Credits

Rachelle Cracchiolo, M.S.Ed., *Publisher*
Conni Medina, M.A.Ed., *Managing Editor*
Nika Fabienke, Ed.D., *Series Developer*
June Kikuchi, *Content Director*
Seth Rogers, *Editor*
Michelle Jovin, M.A., *Assistant Editor*
Lee Aucoin, *Senior Graphic Designer*

TIME For Kids and the TIME For Kids logo are registered trademarks of TIME Inc. Used under license.

Image Credits: p.4 Kristin Callahan/ACE/Newscom; pp.6–7 Eddie Gerald/ Alamy Stock Photo; p.8 Derek Storm/Everett Collection/Alamy Live News; p.10 (inset) Entertainment Pictures/Alamy Stock Photo; p.12 (inset) Everett Collection, Inc./Alamy Stock Photo; pp.12–13 ZUMA Press, Inc./ Alamy Stock Photo; p.14 (inset) Nancy Stone/MCT/Newscom; pp.14–15 Moviestore collection Ltd/Alamy Stock Photo; pp.16–17 Atlaspix/Alamy Stock Photo; p.17 (inset) Kris Connor/Getty Images for The Weinstein Company; pp.18, 19 Illustrations by Timothy J. Bradley; pp.22–23 Robert Gilhooly/Alamy Stock Photo; p.22 (inset) Featureflash Photo Agency/ Shutterstock.com; p.26 Kris Connor/Getty Images for The Weinstein Company; p.30 (inset) Richard Levine/Alamy Stock Photo; pp.30–31 ZUMA Press, Inc./Alamy Stock Photo; p.40 J. Howard Miller/ZUMA Press/ Newscom; all other images from iStock and/or Shutterstock.

Library of Congress Cataloging-in-Publication Data

Names: Rodgers, Kelly author.
Title: Communicate! : documentaries / Kelly Rodgers.
Description: Huntinton Beach, CA : Teacher Created Materials, 2017. | Includes index.
Identifiers: LCCN 2017023523 (print) | LCCN 2017034886 (ebook) | ISBN 9781425854621 (eBook) | ISBN 9781425849863 (pbk.)
Subjects: LCSH: Documentary films--History and criticism--Juvenile literature.
Classification: LCC PN1995.9.D6 (ebook) | LCC PN1995.9.D6 R5795 2017 (print)
 | DDC 070.1/8--dc23
LC record available at https://lccn.loc.gov/2017023523

Teacher Created Materials

5301 Oceanus Drive
Huntington Beach, CA 92649-1030
http://www.tcmpub.com

ISBN 978-1-4258-4986-3

© 2018 Teacher Created Materials, Inc.

Table of Contents

Playing a Vital Role

Have you ever watched a film that made you think about the lives of others? Or one that made you want to help solve a problem? If so, the film may have been a documentary. These films tell stories about real people and real events. Sometimes, they focus on nature or life in the past. Often, they focus on rights.

The rights of people and animals are the theme of many documentaries. Every person has rights. These are called *human rights*. Making sure animals receive **humane** treatment is called *animal rights*. Documentary **filmmakers** can play key roles in making sure human rights and animal rights are protected. They educate and inspire viewers. They urge them to take action.

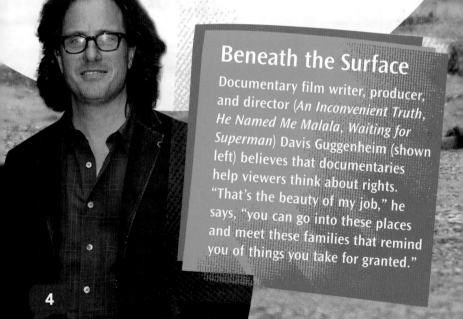

Beneath the Surface

Documentary film writer, producer, and director (*An Inconvenient Truth, He Named Me Malala, Waiting for Superman*) Davis Guggenheim (shown left) believes that documentaries help viewers think about rights. "That's the beauty of my job," he says, "you can go into these places and meet these families that remind you of things you take for granted."

Popular Truth

An Inconvenient Truth is the most popular documentary film ever made. It fights for the rights of all living creatures by making people aware of **climate change**. The film also inspires people to take care of the environment.

The Language of Film

Films are a type of **visual art**. They tell stories through images and film language. Film language is the way all of the sights and sounds of a film impact its overall message. Viewers interpret this language to understand the film's message.

Distinctions

Documentaries, or nonfiction films, are a distinct film **genre**. They record real life. They show real struggles. Films about rights show how humans and animals suffer when their rights are not protected. Humans cannot always stand up for their own rights. Animals cannot speak out for theirs. Documentaries show people how they can help fight for the rights of others.

A Global Declaration

The Universal Declaration of Human Rights (UDHR) was released in 1948 by the United Nations. Though old, it is still an important document. It spells out basic rights for all humans. The UDHR states that all people "are born free and equal in dignity and rights." It includes the rights to life, freedom, and equal protection of the law.

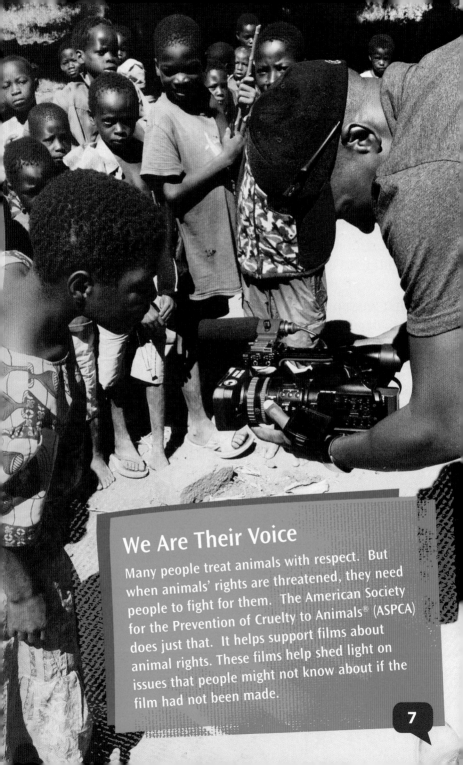

We Are Their Voice

Many people treat animals with respect. But when animals' rights are threatened, they need people to fight for them. The American Society for the Prevention of Cruelty to Animals® (ASPCA) does just that. It helps support films about animal rights. These films help shed light on issues that people might not know about if the film had not been made.

Common Ground

Many documentaries deal with rights. Some films focus on children's rights. These films may focus on bullying in schools or children who have to deal with hunger. Other films shed light on **racism** or **gender discrimination**. And still others show how humans mistreat animals.

Documentaries about rights have certain things in common. They tell stories about people who are fighting to end injustice. They show people who have dealt with these issues firsthand. They show the viewer that anyone can make a difference. And they use film language to **convey** their meanings.

Promoting Love

Lizzie Velasquez (shown left) was born with a disorder that causes her to look different from most people. She was bullied for most of her life. Now, she fights against bullying. Lizzie started her own YouTube channel, which she uses to promote love and hope. The documentary, *A Brave Heart: The Lizzie Velasquez Story*, tells about her life.

Two Sides of the Story

The Elephant in the Living Room focuses on the problems with keeping wild animals as pets. The film shows the struggle to protect the rights of owners and animals. One image in the film shows a lion named Lambert caged in a horse trailer. Seeing a wild animal trapped in a small area stuck in the minds of many viewers.

Stories Are Mirrors

A nonfiction film can help us see ourselves in the story. Personal stories can show how rights issues affect many people. *He Named Me Malala* is about a girl named Malala Yousafzai (mah-LAH-lah yoo-sahf-ZAY). The film connects to viewers through Malala's fight for her right to an education. Viewers see access to school as a basic human right. They can picture themselves in Malala's place.

Shots and Camera Angles

Filmmakers use shots and camera angles to tell their stories. A shot is a single image (like a photograph) that the camera records. When a group of shots are strung together, they create a scene. Many scenes together form a film. In that way, is it similar to a flipbook.

There are different types of shots and camera angles. Each one can convey a unique meaning. For example, a close-up shot of a child's face can make viewers feel attached to the child. A long shot of a child standing alone in a street can make viewers feel sorry for the child. The way the camera is angled can mean things, too. For instance, when a camera looks down on a person in a film, viewers feel like they have the power. When the camera looks up at someone, viewers feel respect for him or her. Filmmakers use these methods to make their **themes** clear.

Setting It Up

A Place at the Table documents the tragic stories of American children who do not have enough to eat. The film opens with some **establishing shots**. These shots show various cities and towns across the United States. They help prepare viewers for the message of the film.

Light and Sound

Filmmakers use special techniques to help make the message of their documentaries clear. These techniques help the viewers grasp the filmmakers' issues. One of these techniques is to use lighting and music to set certain moods. Dark lighting creates a scared or tense mood. Bright lighting creates a hopeful mood. The same is true for sounds. Lights and sounds can make viewers feel things that they might not otherwise.

Narration, or voice-over, is another technique. Voice-overs give the viewers information that they might not know. This helps viewers get a deeper understanding of the events on the screen.

Real Wild

The Elephant in the Living Room uses an unusual technique. Near the end of the film, the filmmaker recorded a scene at a wild animal auction using a hidden camera. The scene shows how people acted when they did not know they were being filmed. This **footage** makes viewers feel as if they are watching something that they should not be seeing.

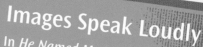

Images Speak Loudly

In *He Named Me Malala*, Malala's voice-overs tell facts about her life and education. At the same time, viewers see a shot of a street in her home country of Pakistan. The street has been blocked. The filmmaker uses the visual to act as a metaphor that shows that the road to equal education in Pakistan is also blocked.

Malala Yousafzai (center), her father Ziauddin (left), and Syrian refugees walk through a Syrian refugee camp.

13

Documentary films have **subjects**, not characters. Sometimes, the subject acts as the film's narrator. This technique gives the film a personal point of view. Subjects help viewers see the world through their eyes. This makes the issue feel real for viewers.

Filmmakers also interview their subjects. This technique lets subjects tell their stories in their own words. They can express their thoughts and feelings. Interviews can take place over hours or even days. Before the interviews make it into the film, filmmakers may have to edit them to make them shorter. In this way, viewers only see what the filmmaker wants them to see.

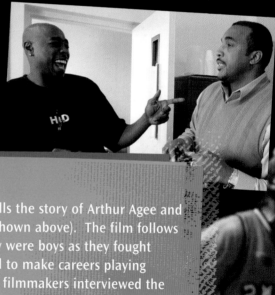

Balanced

Hoop Dreams tells the story of Arthur Agee and William Gates (shown above). The film follows them when they were boys as they fought racism and tried to make careers playing basketball. The filmmakers interviewed the boys, their families, and their friends. These interviews help balance the factual and emotional sides of the film.

Arthur Agee

Real Talks

In *Hoop Dreams*, the filmmakers show old photos of Agee's family. His mother provides a voice-over about the hard life Agee has faced. That works to create a connection between the boys and the viewers. After that, there is a scene of Agee playing basketball. This shows that basketball can pave the way to a better life.

Real or Created?

Some real events are hard to understand. Some filmmakers put words on the screen to help explain events. The text helps move the story along and provides facts. The text can also summarize events that the filmmaker chose to leave out or did not film.

Many nonfiction films use old photos and news articles, too. These tools remind viewers that they are seeing real events. Some films use **reenactments**. Filmmakers can shape these scenes to fit the message of their films. Blurred images and lighting changes are others signs that tell viewers that scenes are reenactments.

Real or Reenacted?

In *Mighty Times: The Children's March*, filmmakers used reenactments of civil rights marches. After the film was released, some viewers did not like the reenactments. They thought the filmmakers should have used actual footage of the marches. But filmmakers argued that they could make images clearer if they reenacted them.

Oprah Winfrey in a civil rights reenactment from the 2014 movie, *Selma*.

Say No to Bullying

Bully follows the lives of five children who are frequently bullied. At different points in the film, photographs and videos of the children when they were younger appear on the screen. These scenes serve to make viewers want to protect these young children from harm.

IT'S TIME TO TAKE A STAND

BULLY

Cracking the Code

Understanding film language helps viewers make sense of what they see. Filmmakers craft each shot to make sure they communicate specific ideas or emotions. Here are some important questions to think about while watching a documentary:

> **camera angle**—Where is the camera positioned, and how does that relate to the subject?

> **depth of focus**—Who/what is closest to the camera? Who/what is farthest from the camera?

lighting—Are there any shadows in the frame? Is the lighting bright or dim?

framing—Who/what is in the shot? Who/what is not in the shot? Where are the subjects placed?

music—Is there music playing? How does it affect what you think? Is there silence? How does what you do or do not hear change what you think?

camera movement—How does the camera move in each shot? Does the camera move quickly or slowly? Does the movement make you think or feel anything?

A Noble Aim

Documentaries have many layers. Film language can help reveal the purpose of the film. Usually, the purpose is to educate viewers about a topic. But many films have more than one purpose. They may also seek to inspire viewers to take action.

Real Power

In 2004, *Super Size Me* showed the negative effects of eating too much fast food. The director of the film, Morgan Spurlock, ate nothing but McDonald's for an entire month. By the end of the month, Spurlock had gained 25 pounds (11.34 kilograms) and developed serious health problems. Viewers were shocked by what they saw. People began to look at fast food in a new light.

All around the world, people fight for their rights. People may hear about a human or animal rights issue. They may see a news program or read an article. But there are still some things that remain unknown. Many nonfiction films focus on these lesser-known events. By shining a light on these issues, filmmakers hope they can make their subjects' lives better.

Food Deserts

A Place at the Table talks about "food deserts." A food desert is a place where fresh food is not available. According to the film, over 23 million Americans live in these places.

Nonfiction films are windows to the world. Films that fight for the rights of others are unique windows. They give viewers a glimpse of the larger world around them. They offer ideas for ways to fight for **social change** and to protect rights. They attempt to motivate viewers to change the way they see the world.

Fighting for Fairness

Zuriel Oduwole (ZUHR-ee-uhl oh-doo-WOHL-ay, shown left) was just nine years old when she made her first film, *The Ghana Revolution*. Her work focuses on issues in Africa. A common theme in her films is the fight for educational rights for girls around the world.

Documentaries are a source of information. They aim to create deeper awareness of rights issues. Filmmakers use facts to provide information. They interview people who fight for a cause to inform viewers. They use graphs and charts, too. All of this helps shed more light on the issue.

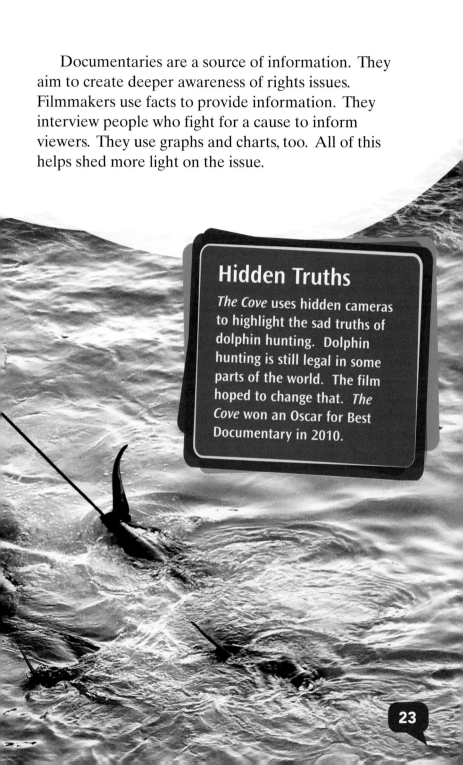

Hidden Truths

The Cove uses hidden cameras to highlight the sad truths of dolphin hunting. Dolphin hunting is still legal in some parts of the world. The film hoped to change that. *The Cove* won an Oscar for Best Documentary in 2010.

A Source of Inspiration

Documentaries inspire viewers. These films show why it is important to stand up for others. They teach people to have **compassion**. They also help people stay informed and introduce them to rights issues.

People who learn more about rights issues are more likely to take a stand for others. Documentaries encourage viewers to do so. These films do this by showing that all humans are connected. Life is not only about personal needs. It is also about caring for each other. Fighting for the rights of others should be part of every life.

Work Together

A Brave Heart: The Lizzie Velasquez Story educates and inspires. The filmmakers show Lizzie **lobbying** in Washington, DC, for the Safe Schools Improvement Act. This law protects victims of school bullying. Lizzie says, "Let's be heard together. Together, let's make a difference."

Inspire Action

In 2014, young people from around the world entered the Action4Climate film competition. These filmmakers focused on the dangers of climate change. They wanted to inspire viewers to do their part in helping the planet.

Documentaries that fight for others' rights also aim to persuade viewers. They try to convince viewers that the issues are important. These films hope that those who watch will relate to their subjects. The goal is to get viewers to change how they see the subjects of the films. If the film is successful, then viewers might get involved.

Anyone can fight to protect the rights of others. Age, strength, and knowledge do not matter. Ordinary people can help ensure the rights of others. Documentaries inspire audiences to make change happen.

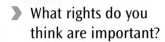

THINK LINK

❯ What rights do you think are important?

❯ How would you use a documentary to showcase your issue?

❯ Which film tools and techniques do you think have the biggest impact on viewers?

Filmmaker Lee Hirsh walks with Kelby Johnson after a screening of *Bully*.

A Global Influence

Kelby Johnson is one of the students featured in the documentary *Bully*. Kelby has faced bullying for many years. Even so, she refuses to move to a different school. In the film, she tells her parents, "If I leave, they win." Kelby's story has inspired many viewers.

A United Pursuit

The Universal Declaration of Human Rights (UDHR) is a document that forms the basis for global human rights law. Nearly every nation in the world agrees with the UDHR, yet human rights abuses still occur.

Some Universal Human Rights

Every person has the right to:

- equality.
- life, liberty, and personal security.
- be recognized as a person under the law.
- equality under the law.
- fair and capable judges to uphold their rights.
- a fair and public hearing.
- be considered innocent until proven guilty.
- free movement.
- protection while in another country.
- a nationality and the freedom to change it.
- marriage and family.

- own property.
- peaceful assembly and association.
- participate in government and elections.
- social security.
- desirable work and to join trade unions.
- rest and leisure.
- adequate living standards.
- education.
- participate in cultural life and responsibilities in the community.
- social order.
- freedom of thought, conscience, and religion.
- freedom of opinion and information.

Every person has freedom from:

- discrimination.
- slavery.
- torture.
- arrest and exile without reason.
- interference with privacy, family, home, and correspondence.

The Key Factor

Filmmakers make documentaries with viewers in mind. The audience fulfills the purpose of the film. They respond to the film language. Filmmakers count on this response. They create content to reach viewers.

Changing Views

Nonfiction films tell stories that challenge viewers. These stories make viewers question what they think, know, and feel. The audience responds to the subjects of the film. The issues, struggles, people, and animals are all subjects. These films inspire viewers to think about how people and animals are treated around the world.

Don't Super Size Me

When viewers saw the poor effects that too much fast food had on Spurlock in *Super Size Me*, they took action. People demanded that McDonald's serve healthier options. Six weeks after the film was released, McDonald's started to phase out its "super size" option.

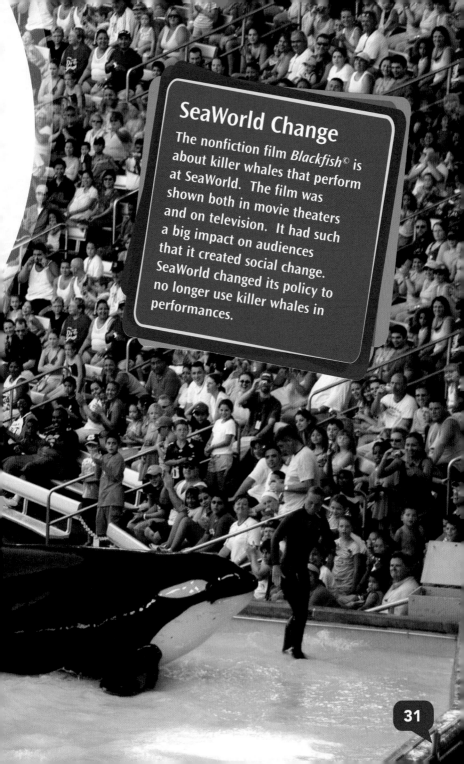

SeaWorld Change

The nonfiction film *Blackfish*© is about killer whales that perform at SeaWorld. The film was shown both in movie theaters and on television. It had such a big impact on audiences that it created social change. SeaWorld changed its policy to no longer use killer whales in performances.

Audience Appeal

Filmmakers know how to connect viewers with issues. They know how to make people think and feel certain ways. Filmmakers use camera angles and music. They use lighting and voice-overs. They do all of this to connect with viewers.

Each image and scene in a nonfiction film is an **appeal**. Filmmakers use appeals to try to persuade viewers to shift their beliefs, feelings, and thoughts. Sometimes, documentaries are hard to watch because they show so much pain. That works as an appeal to viewers to help make a change.

Sit-In

The Dream Is Now follows the lives of four **undocumented** children. In one scene, one of the subjects, Erika, is arrested. She had just staged a **sit-in** at a senator's office. Erika is appealing to the senator to take her rights issues seriously. At the same time, she is appealing to the film's viewers to do the same.

A Heart for Service

Another subject in *The Dream Is Now* is Alejandro. He has spent his whole life wanting to be a Marine. But because he is undocumented, he cannot serve in the military. When Alejandro speaks to filmmakers about his situation, he begins to cry. "Why try if I can't get there, or if I will never get there?" he asks.

Filmmakers use three main types of appeals: *ethos,* *logos,* and *pathos.* When all three are used together in an effective way, filmmakers can connect with viewers in meaningful ways.

Ethos appeals to the beliefs of the viewers. Do the images and people speaking have authority? Is the message in the film realistic?

Logos appeals to viewers' reason. Does the film have real facts? Is the message clear?

Pathos appeals to viewers' emotions. Does the film inspire them? Do the images make them feel a certain way? Does the story inspire them to take action?

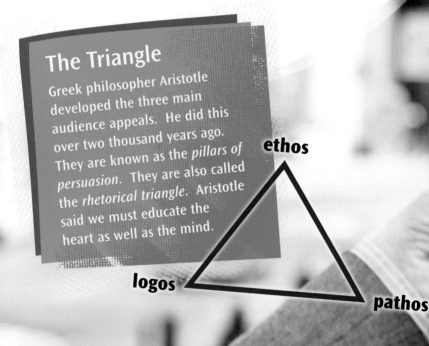

The Triangle

Greek philosopher Aristotle developed the three main audience appeals. He did this over two thousand years ago. They are known as the *pillars of persuasion.* They are also called the *rhetorical triangle.* Aristotle said we must educate the heart as well as the mind.

ethos

logos

pathos

Women in Media

Miss Representation is a film about the way in which women are shown in the **media**. The first shot of the film shows a quote from author Alice Walker: "The most common way people give up their power is by thinking they don't have any." The next shot shows data about how much time teenagers spend interacting with media. The first quote from the author appeals to viewers' pathos and ethos. The data appeals to viewers' logos.

35

A Better Chance

Audience members have a purpose. As they watch a documentary, they question what they see and hear. Viewers interpret the message in the images and respond to the appeals in the film. The viewer can be a key factor in protecting the rights of others.

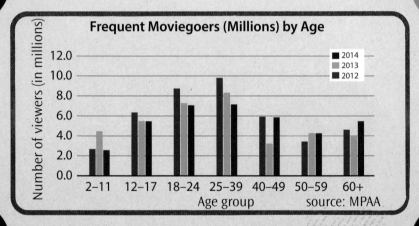

Frequent Moviegoers (Millions) by Age

source: MPAA

Who's Watching?

Filmmakers know they need to reach certain audiences with their content, messages, and presentations. People between the ages of 18 and 39 make up the largest **demographic** of moviegoers. Filmmakers know that fact. So they try to appeal to that age group. They keep those people in mind when they are crafting the language of their films.

Documentaries are meaningless without an audience. When viewers respond to these films, there is a better chance of finding solutions to the issues in question. This is how change takes place. Viewers respond by standing up and speaking out. They respond by joining the fight for the rights of others.

STOP! THINK...

Filmmakers need an audience to connect with their message to be effective. Use the graph on the previous page to help you answer the following questions:

> What age group will most filmmakers try to appeal to?

> How does the audience fulfill the filmmaker's purpose?

> Why does the number of moviegoers in each age group change from year to year?

What Can You Do?

Nonfiction filmmakers want your help. They want you to stay informed, donate money, and get involved with issues. Many organizations need young people to help. Social change often begins with youth.

Do you care about injustice around the world? Try joining a global movement of over 5 million young people making positive change with rights issues.

www.dosomething.org/

Are the rights of animals and the environment your passion? Help protect those without a voice.

www.onegreenplanet.org/

Does your school support the Safe Schools Improvement Act? Learn more about this campaign to stop bullying and make your voice heard by writing to politicians.

www.hrc.org/

Do you know of issues in your community? Make a documentary of your own to help protect the rights of others. Be sure to decide on the purpose, create the language, and find how you will appeal to your specific demographic before filming.

www.minimoviemakers.com

A Better Place

Documentary filmmakers have many roles. They are reporters and **advocates**. They are **activists** and explorers. But most important, they are storytellers. They aim to make people aware of issues. By making these films, they fight for the rights of others.

Documentaries speak through images and film language tools. They appeal to the viewers' emotions. After the film is over, it is up to audience members to create meaning from the film's language and purpose. It is then that documentaries fulfill their purpose of causing social change to happen.

Seeing Change

Miss Representation leads viewers to fight for change. Some people use Twitter™ to point out when they see bad images of women in media. Others send out weekly e-mails. These e-mails keep subscribers up-to-date on things they can do to help change how women are shown in media.

What It Means

After seeing *An Inconvenient Truth*, 9 out of 10 viewers said it made them more aware of climate change. People saw the impact climate change could have on both humans and animals. Since the film's release, new forms of energy, such as solar and wind, have come into use. And over 1 million electric cars have been sold around the world.

Glossary

activists—people who use or support strong actions to change things

advocates—people who support causes

appeal—a serious request for help or support

climate change—changes in Earth's weather patterns

compassion—a feeling of wanting to help another person or animal

convey—to make something known to someone

demographic—a group of people that has a set of qualities in common

establishing shots—types of film shots that tell viewers where and when the scene is taking place

filmmakers—people, such as producers or directors, who make movies

footage—scenes recorded on film or video

gender discrimination—the practice of unfairly treating a person or group of people differently based on whether they are male or female

genre—a certain category or type of art

humane—kind or gentle to animals or people

lobbying—trying to influence government officials to make decisions for or against something

media—radio stations, TV stations, newspapers, and films through which information is delivered to the public

racism—unfair treatment of people because of their race

reenactments—events that have been acted out again

sit-in—a protest where a group of people sit or stay in a place and refuse to leave

social change—a shift in the way people act and think about a particular topic

subjects—people or things shown in works of art

themes—the main subjects described or discussed

undocumented—a person who does not have the official documents that are needed to enter, live in, or work in a country legally

visual art—a work of art that relies on sight, such as drawing, painting, and film

Index

Check It Out!

Books

International Amnesty. 2015. *We Are All Born Free: The Universal Declaration of Human Rights in Pictures.* Francis Lincoln Ltd.

McLaughlin, Danielle. 2016. *That's Not Fair! Getting to Know Your Rights and Freedoms.* CitizenKid.

Videos

An Inconvenient Truth. 2006. Lawrence Bender Productions and Participant Media. PG.

A Place at the Table. 2012. Motto Pictures and Participant Media. PG.

Mighty Times: The Children's March. 2004. HBO Family. NR.

Super Size Me. 2004. The Con and Kathbur Pictures. PG.

The Elephant in the Living Room. 2010. NightFly Entertainment. PG.

Websites

Kids Go Global. www.kidsgoglobal.net

Kid World Citizen. www.kidworldcitizen.org/

Mini Movie Makers. www.minimoviemakers.com

Youth for Human Rights: Making Human Rights a Global Reality. www.youthforhumanrights.org/

Try It!

Imagine you are a documentary filmmaker. Choose an issue that is important to you and plan your film.

⭐ Which issue will you focus on?

⭐ Who will be your target audience? Be sure to keep that demographic's interests in mind when you choose a topic.

⭐ Research your topic. Gather data that shows why your issue is important.

⭐ Draw a scene from your film and label subjects, landmarks, and other important things.

⭐ Write a voice-over for the first scene of your film. Be sure to use words that will grab viewers' attention.

About the Author

Kelly Rodgers lives in Georgia with her family. She teaches middle school and high school history. When Rodgers is not teaching, she likes to read historical fiction novels. Rodgers also likes learning about the lives of the presidents. During summers, she likes traveling to new places. Rodgers enjoys seeing how other people live around the world. She does this in part by watching some of her favorite documentaries.

Showdown

Animal Defenses

Jennifer Kroll

Publishing Credits

Rachelle Cracchiolo, M.S.Ed., *Publisher*
Conni Medina, M.A.Ed., *Managing Editor*
Nika Fabienke, Ed.D., *Series Developer*
June Kikuchi, *Content Director*
John Leach, *Assistant Editor*
Kevin Pham, *Graphic Designer*

TIME For Kids and the TIME For Kids logo are registered trademarks of TIME Inc. Used under license.

Image Credits: Cover and p.1 _548901005677/Getty Images; pp.4–5 Roy Toft/National Geographic Creative; p.18 INTERFOTO/Alamy Stock Photo; p.19 (top) Universal Images Group North America LLC/Alamy Stock Photo; p.24 Michel Gunther/Science Source; p.25 John Serrao/Science Source; all other images from iStock and/or Shutterstock.

Library of Congress Cataloging-in-Publication Data

Names: Kroll, Jennifer L., author.
Title: Showdown : animal defenses / Jennifer Kroll.
Description: Huntington Beach, CA : Teacher Created Materials, [2018] | Audience: Grade 4 to 6. | Includes index.
Identifiers: LCCN 2017017375 (print) | LCCN 2017030008 (ebook) | ISBN 9781425853570 (eBook) | ISBN 9781425849832 (pbk.)
Subjects: LCSH: Animal defenses—Juvenile literature.
Classification: LCC QL759 (ebook) | LCC QL759 .K76 2018 (print) | DDC 591.47--dc23
LC record available at https://lccn.loc.gov/2017017375 Library of Congress Cataloging-in-Publication Data

Teacher Created Materials

5301 Oceanus Drive
Huntington Beach, CA 92649-1030
http://www.tcmpub.com

ISBN 978-1-4258-4983-2

© 2018 Teacher Created Materials, Inc.

Table of Contents

Face Off!

Lions gather at a water hole in Africa. As a rhinoceros steps out of the water, a lioness springs. Her claws grip the rhino's back. But the rhino spins and shakes her off. With its horn lowered, it charges the lions. The lions back away and scatter.

Getting Defensive

It is dangerous out there! Animals have amazing ways of surviving when faced with a scary showdown. Some creatures, such as rhinos, have powerful bodies and sharp horns. Other animals defend themselves with claws, teeth, or speed.

All Together Now

Many animals live and work in groups to stay safer. Musk oxen stand side by side in a circle when threatened by wolves or other **predators**. They keep their calves safe in the center of the circle.

A Quick Escape

The pronghorn uses its speed to escape predators. Pronghorns can run 40 miles (64 kilometers) an hour. That is as fast as cars on the road!

Armored Animals

It takes thick skin to shake off a lion attack. That is exactly what a rhino has. Its tough skin acts like a suit of armor. Rhino skin can be up to 2 inches (5 centimeters) thick. It is made of layers of collagen. This substance is also found in human skin, bones, and tendons. The collagen layers crisscross each other, making the skin super strong.

Other animals also sport "armor" of some kind. Turtles and tortoises have protective shells. A pangolin is covered in tough scales. It defends itself by curling up into a scaly ball. Armadillos use this same trick to **foil** predators.

Borrowed Armor

Hermit crabs are not born with shells. Instead, they find and move into abandoned seashells. When they outgrow a shell, they find a bigger one. Hermit crabs carry their shell homes around with them to stay safe.

white rhinoceros

nine-banded armadillo

box turtle

pangolin

7

Outback Armor

A falcon circles over the Australian **outback**. It spots a small lizard. It's lunchtime! The falcon swoops. The would-be **prey** is no ordinary lizard. It is a thorny dragon, covered in sharp spikes. Under attack, the lizard puffs up its chest. The falcon decides that this lizard might be too much trouble. The bird flies off to seek its meal elsewhere.

Many lizards have armor-like skin. Thorny dragons are a **striking** example. These Australian reptiles have another cool defense. Each dragon has a spiky, knob-like "false head" on its neck. When it tucks its head down, the false head sticks out. Predators see the false head and the tucked head and think the lizard is larger than it really is.

Drop It and Run!

Some animals can drop parts of their bodies to escape from a predator. This is called *autotomy* (uh-TAW-tuh-mee). This is the case for dormice, wolf spiders, and geckos. When these animals are under attack, they **sacrifice** something to get away.

Dormouse

Dormice are relatives of mice and squirrels. The skin on a dormouse's tail is very thin. It can break off easily if a predator grabs it. This allows the dormouse to escape. Afterward, the skinless portion of the tail falls off. The lost tail (or tail section) does not grow back.

Wolf Spider

All spiders have eight legs, but only some of them can lose legs easily. Wolf spiders hunt without webs. When grabbed by a predator, the legs of these spiders can come off to let them run away. Younger spiders can even regrow the leg they lose.

Gecko

Geckos' tails are divided into sections. Between each section is a *fracture zone*, an area where the tail can easily break apart. When geckos are in danger, their tails may simply fall off. The dropped tails continue wiggling, which can distract predators. Geckos grow back their lost tails.

Now You See It

A dark shadow moves through the water above a coral reef. It's a shark! A cuttlefish senses that it is in danger. This small, squid-like creature cannot hope to outpace the much larger predator. The cuttlefish's body begins to change color rapidly. Its skin becomes the same shade as the nearby coral. Its extended arms look like coral branches. The cuttlefish has such good **camouflage** that the shark swims right by.

Cuttlefish are masters of disguise. They can change their appearance at will. This ability helps them escape predators. It also helps them catch prey and impress potential mates.

Not a True Fish

A cuttlefish is a mollusk, not a fish. A mollusk is an animal with a soft body and no spine. Squid, clams, octopuses, and snails are all mollusks.

Clever Cuttlefish

Cuttlefish have large brains and are very smart. Scientists have shown that cuttlefish can solve problems and learn maze patterns.

Blending In

There are a few other animals like cuttlefish. Chameleons, squid, and octopuses can change colors quickly, too.

Many other animals use camouflage for defense. Instead of changing colors, they blend into their environment. Snowshoe hares have white fur in winter. This helps them blend in with the snow. The speckled coats of young white-tailed deer help them stay hidden in the forest.

"Leaf "Me Alone

A dead leaf floats to the ground, but it flies away before it lands. Surprise! It is actually a living dead-leaf butterfly. Predators needs sharp eyes to spot this insect.

Other insects use the same kind of camouflage. Leaf insects look just like the leaves they eat. Stick insects resemble twigs.

See a Dragon?

It may look like floating seaweed, but those "weeds" are really a leafy sea dragon. These relatives of sea horses live off the coast of Australia.

snowshoe hare

Praying Mantis

Praying mantises are insects that have many types of camouflage. Some mantises look like flowers to lure bugs into their clutches. Another mantis species looks a lot like an ant. This keeps it safe from predators that avoid ants.

Super Squid Defenses

Like cuttlefish, squid change color to blend in and hide. Here are some of their other amazing defenses.

An Inky Escape

Inside a squid's body is a sac full of ink. Squid can shoot this ink out through their siphons (SY-fuhns). The ink cloud startles predators. It blocks their view and distracts them, giving the squid time to escape.

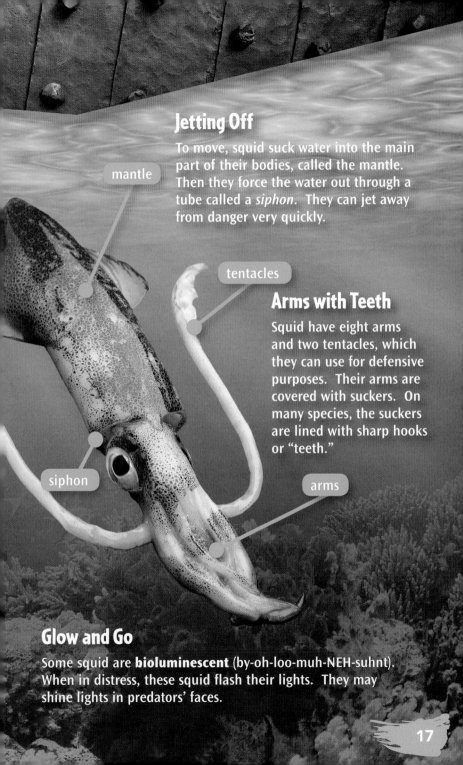

Jetting Off

To move, squid suck water into the main part of their bodies, called the mantle. Then they force the water out through a tube called a *siphon*. They can jet away from danger very quickly.

mantle

tentacles

Arms with Teeth

Squid have eight arms and two tentacles, which they can use for defensive purposes. Their arms are covered with suckers. On many species, the suckers are lined with sharp hooks or "teeth."

siphon

arms

Glow and Go

Some squid are **bioluminescent** (by-oh-loo-muh-NEH-suhnt). When in distress, these squid flash their lights. They may shine lights in predators' faces.

Keep-Away Spray

A hungry wolf spider spots a bombardier beetle. It moves toward its prey and is ready to pounce.

Bang! A loud sound startles the spider. A boiling spray hits its legs and eyes. The spray not only burns but smells terrible. Bang! The foul spray explodes from the beetle's body again. The wolf spider turns and scurries away.

Bombardier beetles shoot hot, smelly spray out of **glands** in their backsides. The spray is a mixture of two **chemicals**. These are kept in two separate chambers in their bodies. When the beetles sense danger, the chemicals flow together. Mixed together, they heat up and explode!

Bombs Away

How did the bombardier beetle get its name? Bombardiers were U.S. Air Force members. They dropped bombs from planes during World War II.

Feeling the Burn

A bombardier beetle's spray is boiling hot. It is more than 212°F (100°C)! The beetle can shoot this spray up to 20 times in a row.

bombardier beetle

Black-and-White Warning

Who needs armor, speed, or camouflage? Skunks have none of these defenses. Yet they are preyed upon by few animals.

Like bombardier beetles, skunks defend themselves by spraying a stinky liquid. Their spray can travel up to 9.8 feet (3 meters). People can smell this spray from more than a mile away.

Often, though, skunks do not need to spray. Predators see their black and white stripes and know to steer clear. Skunks have what is called a "warning **coloration**."

Striped polecats have the same coloration. These weasel relatives live in Africa. Like skunks, polecats defend themselves with spray that smells horrible!

Defending the Nest

Green wood hoopoes make a spray that smells like rotten eggs. The birds use the spray around their nest to keep predators away.

❯ Can you think of any other animals with a warning coloration? (Hint: It does not have to be black and white.)

❯ Great horned owls often prey on skunks. These predators lack one of the five senses. Can you guess which one?

❯ Skunks prefer to avoid using up their spray. What might a skunk do to avoid spraying?

Playing Dead

It is dusk, and a Virginia opossum wanders through a clearing. Another animal is looking for dinner, too. The opossum spots a coyote. Danger!

The opossum does not run. Instead, it falls down and "plays dead." Its mouth hangs open, and its **limbs** become stiff. The coyote ignores the "dead" opossum and continues on its way.

Many predators only attack living and moving prey. This is why some animals play dead as a defense. Opossums can keep up the act for hours. To see if the danger has passed, they move their ears to listen for other animals. Once they know they are safe, they get right back to what they were doing.

Sick Trick

Opossums sometimes fake being sick. They drool and try to look weak and ill. This works because predators tend to avoid sick prey.

A Snake Fake Out

The eastern hognose snake is another species that plays dead. When frightened, these snakes roll onto their backs with their mouths open. While in this position, they sometimes vomit. It is unclear why the snakes do this. It could be that the sight of the vomit, which could include a poisonous toad or newt, might scare off predators. These snakes are **immune** to the poison. It might be that vomiting lightens their stomachs so the snakes can flee.

Hognose snakes are great actors! Besides playing dead, they have other defenses, too. They can release a foul-smelling fluid from scent glands. They also have mildly **venomous** bites, though the venom is not very dangerous to humans.

Named for Its Nose

The hognose snake got its name from its nose. Its turned-up nose looks a little like a pig snout. Hognose snakes are nicknamed "puff adders" because they puff themselves up to look fierce.

Survival

Animals are amazing. They use different defenses to survive. Some stay safe by playing dead. Others have armor-like skin. Some use camouflage to hide from danger. Others blast predators with smelly spray.

Animals in one area may have many ways to protect themselves. Animals in another place may just have a few defenses. This is because they face different dangers.

What natural defenses do humans have? How did our **ancestors** stay safe from predators? These defenses affect our lives now in a different way than in the past. What would you do if you were faced with a sudden, scary showdown?

A Change of Defense

Many animals use more than one form of defense. They may use these defenses at different times. They may change methods of defense as they go through their life cycles.

caterpillar and monarch butterfly

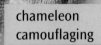
chameleon
camouflaging

The Landscape of Escape

Animals choose their home turfs with defense in mind. They select spots that can help keep them safe. Trees, rocks, sand, and water might be used as hiding places or safety zones.

Glossary

ancestors—relatives who lived long ago

bioluminescent—able to glow in the dark

camouflage—a disguise that allows one to blend in, or the act of blending in

chemicals—certain kinds of liquids or gases

coloration—patterns or colors on an animal

foil—to stop someone's plan

glands—parts of the body that release fluids

immune—not affected by

limbs—a person's or animal's arms, legs, or wings

outback—a desert-like part of Australia where few people live

predators—animals that hunt for and eat other animals

prey—an animal that is hunted and killed for food; to hunt for food

sacrifice—to give up something that is valued

striking—attracting attention by being remarkable

venomous—having a toxic bite or sting

Index

Check It Out!

Books

Grambo, Rebecca. 1997. *Amazing Animals: Defenses*. Kidsbooks, Inc.

Helman, Andrea. 2008. *Hide and Seek: Nature's Best Vanishing Acts*. Walker Childrens.

Kaner, Etta. 1999. *Animal Defenses: How Animals Protect Themselves*. Kids Can Press.

Wilsdon, Christina. 2009. *Animal Defenses*. Chelsea House.

Yaw, Valerie. 2011. *Color-Changing Animals*. Bearport Publishing.

Video

Ultimate Wildlife: Animal Defense. Columbia River Entertainment.

Websites

PBS. *Wild Kratts*. www.pbskids.org/wildkratts/.

Smithsonian Education. *Here's Looking at You, Squid*. www.smithsonianeducation.org/families/point_click/activitysheets/si_activity_squid.pdf.

Try It!

What is your favorite animal? Draw or print out a picture of the animal. Write a description of it by answering the questions below. If you do not know the answers, do some research online or in a library.

🐾 Where does this animal live?

🐾 What are its daily habits?

🐾 Which predators pose a threat to this animal?

🐾 What other threats does it face?

🐾 How does the animal stay safe? What kinds of defenses does it use?

🐾 On your picture, label the parts of the animal that help it defend itself.

About the Author

Jennifer Kroll is the author of 20 books for kids and teachers. She used to write and edit *Read*, a classroom magazine for students. Kroll likes to learn and write about science. She lives in Connecticut with her husband and two children. Kroll thinks her sense of humor is her best defense. However, she doubts it would help in case of an attack by a humorless polar bear.